ALBERT EINSTEIN
and the Theory of Relativity

SOLUTIONS

◆

ALBERT EINSTEIN
and the Theory of Relativity

BY ROBERT CWIKLIK
Illustrated by T. Lewis

BARRON'S

First edition published 1987
by Barron's Educational Series, Inc.

© Copyright 1987 by Eisen, Durwood & Co., Inc.
Cover art by Daniel Maffia
Illustrated by T. Lewis

All inquiries should be addressed to:
Barron's Educational Series, Inc.
250 Wireless Blvd.
Hauppauge, NY 11788

Library of Congress Catalog Card No. 87-19549

International Standard Book No. 0-8120-3921-1

Library of Congress Cataloging-in-Publication Data

Cwiklik, Robert.
    Albert Einstein and the theory of relativity.

    (Solutions)
    Bibliography.
    Includes index.
    Summary: Traces the life and work of the physicist whose theory of
relativity revolutionized scientific thinking.
    1. Einstein, Albert, 1879–1955—Biography—Juvenile
literature.   2. Relativity (Physics)—Juvenile
literature.   [1. Einstein, Albert, 1879–1955.
2. Physicists]   I. Title.   II. Series: Solutions (New
York, N.Y.)
QC16.E5C88   1987   530.1'1   [92]   87-19549
ISBN 0-8120-3921-1

Printed in the United States of America

19 18 17 16 15 14 13 12 11

CONTENTS

CHAPTER ONE

In a Flash of Light

The city of Munich, Germany, had always been the sort of place one reads about in storybooks. It had huge castles and great kings, bronze statues and grassy squares. It was a festive place whose people were famous for making delicious sausages and pastries and for brewing fine beer.

The happy people of Munich would use just about any excuse to have a celebration. On one night, in the year 1883, there was a good reason for one, for a strange and wonderful event was about to happen. Electric lights, long the rage in many parts of the world, would finally brighten a building in Munich for the first time.

By sundown on that night a large crowd of people had gathered in front of the Residenztheater, the city's oldest and grandest theater. Among them was the Einstein family. The Einsteins were very interested in what was about to happen, and they arrived early to get a spot with a good view. Four-year-old Albert Einstein probably had the best view of all. His father lifted the boy up onto his broad shoulders, so that Albert could see everything that was happening.

Albert's father, Hermann Einstein, and Albert's uncle Jacob were probably more excited than most people in Munich were on this night. Even though Hermann looked like an "Old World" gentleman, with his jolly, round face and bushy handlebar mustache, he was involved in the most modern affairs of the day. He and his brother Jacob owned an electrical equipment shop. The coming of electric lights to Munich could mean more business for them. They felt that once people saw the marvel of electric lights, they would soon want them in all the buildings in town, even in their own homes.

From atop his father's shoulders, Albert could see more crowds of people arriving as darkness approached. They came in horse-drawn carriages and on foot. People were milling about in the broad avenue and spilling onto the grass of the great squares. They talked and laughed gaily and loudly while an oom-pah band played, and glockenspiels jangled in the background. Weisswurst and bratwurst and all of the famous Munich sausages cooked on the spit. Their odor spread over everything in wisps of smoke. Men in leather knee-breeches clacked mugs of sudsy beer. Women dressed in colorful dirndls kept the children in line.

As the celebration wound on, darkness fell. Everyone sensed that the event they were waiting for was about to happen. The crowd grew tense with excitement.

Suddenly, the gas lamps along the avenue were dimmed. The street was almost totally dark. The band stopped playing. The people grew so quiet that they could

Electric light celebration, Munich.

hear the sausages roasting. Then, from somewhere un-
seen, a switch was thrown.

In a great flash, the huge theater exploded in a blaze
of bright, white light. The light spilled onto the crowd.
The horses in the avenue shied and dogs yelped and
howled, startled by the sudden brightness. But the people
raised up a great cheer and began to applaud loudly. They
stared at the theater in astonishment and wonder.

All around the theater building lamps were burning—not with smoky wicks and gas, but with clean, new
electric lights. They glowed from the large awning that
covered the entrance. They shone around the huge mar-
quee announcing the night's entertainment. They blazed
forth from every window in every room, pouring bright,
smokeless light onto the sidewalk and far out into the
avenue beyond.

The crowd cheered louder and louder as the oom-pah band struck up again. Beer flowed more freely than before. People filled large, foamy mugs to raise in a toast to the marvel they had seen. It almost seemed as if a new and more exciting world had been born in a flash of light, sweeping away the homely traditions of their storybook city.

The round, staring faces of the crowd reflected the light like so many tiny moons. One of the staring faces belonged to young Albert. He was fascinated by the power of electricity, the way it could light an entire building with just the flick of a switch.

When Albert was a little boy in Munich, electric power had already been brought to many of the world's cities, and electric devices—some of them quite strange—were becoming very chic. Besides electric lights and appliances, which were of course quite useful, people were selling and buying all sorts of electric oddities. There were electric garters to improve posture, electric cigarettes that could be lit without matches, electric combs to control stubborn hair, and even electric necktie lights to give a fashionable glow to a suit of clothes.

Although ordinary people were starting to use electricity in their everyday lives in many ways, they didn't really understand how it worked. They viewed it as a sort of miracle. Even scientists were baffled by some of the things they were discovering about electricity.

In one experiment, conducted around the turn of the century, scientists ran an electric current through a vacuum tube to create a cathode ray. They discovered that these rays were made up of a beam of particles which they called electrons. Electrons are so small that trillions of them could fit on the point of a pin. Everything contains electrons. Each electron has an electric charge. When many electrons are moving in the same direction through a wire, there is an electric current in the wire.

Hendrik Lorenz, a well-known physicist, had developed a complicated mathematical theory about electrons. One point in his theory was the strange idea that at very high speeds, the mass of the electron would get bigger. For centuries physicists had had the firm idea that every object has a definite mass which does not change. Heavy objects have more mass than light ones. The mass is measured by how hard it is to change the motion of the object: to make it speed up, slow down, or change direction. We know a golf ball has more mass than a ping-pong ball, because it is a lot harder to stop a flying golf ball. Lorenz thought that the mass of an electron increases at very high speeds because of its electric charge.

In a cathode ray tube, like the picture tube of your television set, electrons travel at enormous speeds, nearly the speed of light. Light travels at 186,000 miles a second, fast enough for a beam of light to go around the earth eight times in a second. When an experiment was done to test Lorenz's theory, it was found that the mass of the electrons in a cathode ray did in fact increase.

As a grown man Albert Einstein was not satisfied with the theory that explained the mass increase of the electron. He thought that it had nothing to do with charge, and that even uncharged objects would show this mass increase. Some other questions were puzzling the physicists of that day: When the light from a star passes through a telescope, why is it not affected by the motion of the earth? Where does all the energy of radioactive materials come from? How is it possible for the sun to burn for billions of years without running out of fuel? Why does the planet Mercury travel in an orbit that seems to be a little wrong?

While he was still a young man, Einstein gave the world a new theory that answered all these questions, and many others that had not yet appeared. He changed forever the way people think about the universe.

When Albert got home after the celebration, exhausted and drowsy, he didn't look like a child who would one day solve the riddles of the universe, or any riddle for that matter. Even when Albert was born, on March 14, 1879, his mother felt that something might be wrong with him. He had a very large head that was oddly shaped. Albert took much longer to learn to talk than did other children, and his parents feared he might be retarded.

When Albert did learn to talk, he never really said much. He talked mostly to his sister Maja, but since she was only two years old, such conversations could never amount to much. Even this evening, though he had been watchful throughout the exciting celebration, he had remained strangely quiet and aloof.

As Albert undressed sleepily, the housekeeper came in to check on him. She liked to chide Albert, to try to make him talk more. "Did Father Bore enjoy himself this evening?" she asked. Albert just shrugged his shoulders and didn't say a word.

"Father Bore" was a nickname the housekeeper had given to Albert for being so quiet and aloof. She wasn't trying to hurt his feelings, but she felt that it wasn't normal for a little boy to be so quiet. Albert almost felt like explaining to her that one didn't have to talk a lot to enjoy oneself. But he kept quiet. The chatty housekeeper would never understand anyway.

Downstairs, Jacob sat before the fire and spoke loudly to his brother about the new dynamo he was designing. A dynamo is a machine that generates electricity, and soon there would be a great demand for them. Jacob's job in the family business was to invent new electrical devices. He had a real talent for inventing. Tonight, his mind was racing with new ideas for electrical inventions to make the Einstein family rich—and perhaps even famous.

Meanwhile, Hermann was busy counting in his head the number of arc-lamps that were left in the shop. Surely they would sell out soon. Hermann's job was to keep track of the inventory and the books. He didn't have his brother's talent for inventing things, but he was a good businessman who got along with everyone.

Albert's mother, Pauline, thought that all of this talk might be keeping the children awake. But tonight she was being a little more patient than usual with her husband and brother-in-law. She knew how important the demonstration had been to them. But she couldn't help worrying that maybe they were getting their hopes up too high.

Pauline was a beautiful woman who wore her hair piled high on her head. She had a broad, turned-up nose that made her look quite dignified. Pauline tended to worry more than her husband, who never seemed to have a care in the world. But she knew she had to believe in Hermann if the business was ever to succeed.

Albert's home was seldom a quiet place. His father and uncle were constantly discussing their inventions and business prospects late into the night. The sound of music and singing could often be heard in the Einstein living room. Pauline was an excellent pianist, and everyone in the family loved to sing. Although the house did tend to be noisy, it was a happy home, and Albert felt very secure there.

On the morning of Albert's first day of school his mother was worried about him. He seemed so listless and unhappy. She watched him as he stood in the doorway getting ready to walk to school with his father.

Albert was moving very slowly. He took a long time tying his shiny, new school shoes, lacing them so tightly his mother thought they might never come off. He buttoned his new blazer sluggishly and methodically. Obviously, Pauline thought, he was in no hurry to get off to school. He seemed to think that it was not a place he would enjoy.

On the walk to school Albert and his father came upon many other fathers who were walking their sons

First day at school.

and daughters to school. Hermann greeted all the people they met with a sunny smile and a hearty "Good morning." He knew almost everyone in the town, and had something to say to everyone. People must have thought it odd that this good-natured, outgoing man should be the father of shy Albert, who practically hid behind his father when someone passed by.

When Albert and his father arrived at the schoolhouse there was a crowd of little children in the playground outside. The little girls were huddled together in a corner, giggling, and admiring each other's new school dresses and skirts. The little boys were all wearing new blazers and knickerbockers to school, but that didn't stop them from running and playing games.

Albert said goodbye to his father and walked slowly onto the playground with the other children. Instead of joining the other boys in their games, he went and stood next to the schoolhouse with the girls.

When a couple of the boys raced over and asked Albert to join in their game of tag, Albert simply smiled and said, "No, thank you." He didn't enjoy playing sports and roughhousing. He had a different nature than most little boys; he preferred to stand by and observe things. The boys didn't say anything, but they did think it was a little strange that Albert was standing around with *girls* when he could be running and playing.

There was certainly no playing inside the classroom. The schools in Germany were very strict when Albert was a boy. The first thing that Albert's class learned was how to stand up all together when the teacher entered the room and respectfully say, "Good morning." The next thing they learned was not to sit down until the teacher said to, and then all were to sit down at the same time.

There were many other such rules of the classroom that Albert and his fellow students learned. They also learned that a child who broke the rules received swift punishment—often a smack on the wrist or a whack across the shins with a heavy wooden cane. The classroom itself was as stern and harsh as the teaching. The benches the children sat on were made of hard wood. The backs of the benches were stiff and straight, and it was impossible to sit comfortably in them. They were designed to be uncomfortable so that student's wouldn't relax too much in class. That would lead to daydreaming. Better for students to feel the bite of the hard wooden bench. Being uncomfortable kept the students alert and thinking clearly, or so the school officials thought.

Albert was very unhappy in school. He had been told by his parents that school was a place to learn about ideas and far-away places, so that one's outlook would be stretched and broadened. But Albert's school was not such a place, as even his idealistic and kind parents surely must have known. Knowledge and ideas were not discussed, but memorized and repeated in mindless, monotonous chants, over and over again.

After these boring rehearsals, the children had to repeat the things they learned on a test. Often they had not learned much beyond the skill of repeating the right things at the right times. And this skill they learned only to avoid the sting of the teacher's cane. Instead of broadening the mind, this kind of schooling made the spirit shrink and hide in boredom, and even fear.

Albert despised school. Sometimes he would pretend to be sick to be able to stay at home. But his mother and father, like most parents, were too clever to be fooled by such ruses.

Albert's parents understood how much he disliked going to school, but they had great respect for learning. They wanted their son to get an education, and they also felt that, given the chance, Albert might do well in his studies one day. After all, they thought, he possessed the one gift that is necessary for an education. He was curious about everything. He was always asking his parents and his uncle Jacob question after question about things that puzzled him.

Compass gift.

One day, when Albert really was ill and had stayed home from school, Hermann returned from the shop with a present for his son. Wearing a wide smile that wrinkled the sides of his face, Hermann walked into Albert's room and up to the bed where his son lay huddled under blankets. Then he pulled his fist from behind his back and held it in front of Albert. When Hermann opened his hand, Albert saw in it a device that looked something like a watch. However, there were no numbers on its face, only four letters: *N, E, S* and *W*. There were no hands either, only a needle that jerked when the device was turned.

The instrument was a compass. A compass is used by travelers to help them determine in which direction they are traveling. Hermann explained to his wide-eyed son that the wonderful thing about a compass is that, no matter which way you turn it, the needle always points to the north. And, once you know which way the north

12

is, it is easy to figure out which way south, east, and west are.

Albert suddenly did not seem to be sick at all. He was full of curiosity about the compass and he asked his father a great many questions about it. The main question on his mind was, how does the compass always know which way north is?

Albert's father sat on the bed and explained that the needle of a compass always points north because it is attracted by magnetism to the North Pole. In fact, the earth itself is like a huge magnet, surrounded by a magnetic field that turns compass needles. Albert was fascinated by this strange, invisible force that had been around him all the time, but about which he had never known. He began to wonder what other forces might be hidden in the mysterious and wonderful world of nature.

CHAPTER TWO

Pennies in a Well

A lbert never forgot what his father told him about the compass. It planted in his mind a seed of curiosity about nature that was to blossom and grow all his life long.

On clear nights, Albert would go behind his house to look up at the starry sky. He would stand there, his head bent back, and try to understand his place in the universe and the vast network of tiny, distant stars. He would stand for hours and stare at the twinkling pinpoints of light in the night sky. The stars had a mysterious and powerful hold over Albert. Sometimes he even felt a little like crying when he looked up at them, though he couldn't say just why. The stars and the universe seemed endless. How could humans, with their small minds, even begin to grasp the immensity of the far-flung universe? Albert wondered a lot about this.

Though Albert didn't talk much as a child, he was very sensitive, which is often true of quiet people. He was especially sensitive to ideas. Ideas come into the heads of most people and are soon forgotten, like pennies tossed to the bottom of a murky well. But Albert took the pennies that fell into the deep well of his mind and examined each of them, turning them over and over again in his thoughts. After a while, each little penny of an idea was transformed into part of a larger treasure which became very valuable to him, and eventually to all the world.

Sometimes, when Albert was particularly bored in school, he would allow his mind to wander to thoughts of his compass, or the mystery of magnetism, or one of the hundreds of things he was curious about. At times like this, a smile was likely to bloom on Albert's face. His daydreaming made him happy. It lifted him out of the dull and dusty realm of textbooks and lifeless memorizing into a lofty world of real knowledge and understanding.

Albert often got into trouble for his dreamy ways. Once, during a particularly dull lesson, Albert sat with the familiar musing smile on his face. The teacher halted the class and aimed a stern look at Albert. "I would prefer, Mr. Einstein, that you were not in this class," scolded the teacher. "All you do is sit in that back row and smile, and that destroys the feeling of respect that a teacher deserves from the class."

Albert left school that day feeling very small and sad. He didn't enjoy being branded a troublemaker. After all, he had only been sitting and thinking, not *doing* anything wrong. Was it his fault, Albert wondered, if the teacher was so boring he could put an entire school to sleep? Faced with such a tedious situation, who wouldn't allow his mind to wander a little?

When Albert shuffled slowly past a square on the road home, he noticed a group of soldiers standing in rows in the well-groomed grass. The soldiers were

Dreaming in class.

grouped in front of a great bronze statue of a wild pig. The pig, strong, dumb, and proud, stood with its broad snout flared in anger. The soldiers seemed angry, too, as they ran stern-faced through drills while their sergeant barked commands.

"Right shoulder . . . *arms!*" commanded the sergeant, and all together the soldiers lifted their long rifles, standing them against their shoulders with a harsh slap. Albert's eyes grew wide as he saw the bright sun glinting off the long, sharp bayonets fixed to the ends of the rifles. They could cut a person to pieces. Why on earth, he wondered, would anyone want to use such a thing to harm another person?

Albert watched the soldiers as all together they windmilled their rifles, and rested their rifles, and cocked their rifles, and aimed their rifles, and on and on. The sergeant led the men through one mindless drill after another. A thought struck Albert. This sergeant was very much like his teacher at school. He barked commands and the soldiers obeyed—without smiling. No questions asked. This was exactly how German teachers ran their classes, as if students were a platoon of little soldiers.

Albert scanned the now-crowded square. Other boys on their way home from school had stopped to watch the soldiers. These boys were smiling. They enjoyed looking at the soldiers' bright blue uniforms with their smart brass buttons. The long, steeple-topped domes of the soldiers' helmets were a source of wonder to these young boys, who doubtless wished to be soldiers someday, too. Albert thought these pointy hats looked ridiculous.

All along the avenue a crowd of people had gathered to watch the soldiers. Albert noticed that not only children but grown men and women also stood in awe, looking at the harsh sideshow.

Germany had not always been a place where soldiers were so admired. Once, Germans were a peaceful people, known chiefly as great artists, poets, thinkers, and especially musicians, like the great Bach, Mozart, Beethoven, and Brahms. In recent years, however, Germany had fought bloody wars with some of her close neighbors in Europe. During those times, the German people had grown dependent on the army of the mighty German state of Prussia. The Prussians had always been good soldiers, and they had wanted Germany to "carry a big stick" in the world so that nations would fear and respect her. Now, the Germans were listening.

Soldiers and soldiering were now very popular in Munich and in all of Germany. Mothers and fathers wanted their daughters to marry military officers. People had to get off the sidewalk whenever an officer passed by, to show the proper respect. Businesses were now run like military regiments. Even schools, as Albert had seen, borrowed some of the harsh tactics of the military. No better method of training young people could be imagined than to make them as disciplined as soldiers.

It was thought that every little boy wanted to grow up to wear the colors of a German soldier. Albert thought otherwise. He hated the sternness of his schoolhouse. How much worse an army barracks would be, he thought. There would be no escape from foolish rules and regulations. He wanted no part of it.

Fortunately, Albert could escape from the rigidity of the schoolhouse and the soldiers when he was at home. Albert spent a lot of time playing with his little sister Maja, probably his closest friend as a child. Albert's mother and father tried to include their son in everything they did.

When he was about eight years old, Albert's mother had Albert start taking violin lessons. She wanted her son to learn how music could make life more beautiful and satisfying. Pauline dreamed of playing Mozart on her piano while Albert bowed his violin in accompaniment.

At first, Albert hated his violin lessons. He never liked being forced to learn anything. He was only good at learning things he wanted to learn. In later life, he would say that "love is the best teacher," meaning that if you love a thing, you will be eager to learn about it, and the work will not *seem* hard. Even though Albert didn't *love* practicing the violin, he loved his mother, so he stayed with his music lessons. It paid off, for Albert eventually became a very good violinist. Music, to him, became something of a beloved friend with whom he stayed in touch all his long life.

Albert also spent a lot of time in the busy electrical supply shop of his father and uncle. He loved to explore the curious gadgets and machines that were always strewn about. And he loved to watch Uncle Jacob at the drawing board, a pencil tucked behind his ear, measuring the detailed designs of his new inventions with his protractor and ruler.

One day Albert overheard his father and uncle talking about their latest deal. Business had been good lately, and they had just landed a big contract. The Einstein brothers would install electric lights at the Oktoberfest, the yearly festival that was the most popular celebration in the city. The festival had never before been brightened by electric lights. This was a great opportunity for the Einstein Electrical Equipment Company to show the city of Munich what it could do.

The Oktoberfest was to be held on the fairgrounds outside of town. It was an annual festival, held every October for as long as anyone could remember, to celebrate the new fall harvest. Huge canvas tents were set up to house puppet and magic shows, plays, games of chance and skill, costume contests, and enough good food to feed an army.

Albert was kept busy helping his father and uncle string up lights in all of the tents and around the grounds. Albert helped to carry things from the wagon, while Hermann and Jacob strung wire above the tents to power the lights. The brothers were using their newest dynamo to power the lights at the festivities. They wanted to produce more than enough power. A blackout in the middle of such a festive occasion would be very embarrassing, and could ruin them.

When darkness fell on festival night, the fairgrounds glowed from end to end with the Einsteins' lights. Their lampposts surrounded the tents and dotted the grounds. Every booth and table, inside and outside the tents, sat in a wide pool of light. The bright lamps suffused the sky above with a glow. People on their way to the grounds knew which direction to go—they just walked toward the halo in the sky.

During the festivities, Albert's parents and Uncle Jacob stoked the furnace with coal to keep up the steam that powered the dynamo. They could not let the machine fail them on this night, or their business would surely fail as well. The dynamo did not fail. It kept motoring along smoothly, pumping out all the power the fair needed to stay bright the whole night long.

Albert walked the grounds with Maja, making sure that all the lights were still burning, and taking in some of the fun. Albert could show Maja around the wildest spectacles. He'd been to the fair before, but it was Maja's first trip. Albert laughed when Maja's eyes grew wide with fright as the sword swallower gorged on his long blade, or the fire eater spit out balls of flame. Maja herself laughed at the puppet show. She had never seen one before, and the puppets' costumes and antics made her giggle.

Finally, Albert took Maja to the tent where the main event of the festival took place, the beer drinking contest. Munich is a city that is famous the world over for brewing fine beer. Every Autumn at the Oktoberfest, beer drinkers from all over Europe came to Munich to sample different beers, and see who could guzzle the most fresh brew.

The beer tent was one of the largest. Inside, under the bright, new lights, long tables were set up end to end. The beer drinkers lined up alongside the tables. In front of each of them were two dozen steins brimming with foamy beer. The steins each held a liter, which is a little more than a quart. It takes someone with a very strong stomach—and a very weak brain—to drink that much beer all at once.

Finally, the judge gave the sign and, with a tremendous cheer from the crowd, the drinking began. All along the tables men lifted mug after mug of beer to their lips, tilting their heads back and drinking the beer in deep gulps. The sudsy brew trickled down their chins. As the men guzzled and guzzled, Maja began to look seasick. The men's dopey, drunken faces in the bright, glaring lights disgusted her. When it was over, Maja made Albert swear never to drink beer like that.

At home that night, Albert's mother scolded him for

Beer-drinking contest.

taking Maja to the beer-drinking contest. She thought it was something that no decent person should see, especially a little girl. But Hermann and Jacob were in such a jolly mood that Pauline couldn't stay angry at her son for very long. The Einstein brothers' lighting equipment had been a success. It had provided clean, clear light throughout the festival. Everyone must have seen the sign painted in huge letters on the side of their wagon, parked under the brightest light of all, which read: EINSTEIN ELECTRIC CO. This was a perfect advertisement for the brothers, for it associated the Einstein name with all the joy and excitement of the brightly lit festival. Hermann felt that thereafter when people wanted lights and dynamos, they would contact the Einsteins. "The men who made the Oktoberfest glow," he said.

It looked as if the Einsteins had made their reputation. They hoped that now, businesses in Munich would buy dynamos to channel power and lights to their shops and factories. Maybe residents would even want to wire their homes for electric lights. But the Einstein brothers had some competition. They made dynamos that generated DC power. DC stands for direct current, the kind of current that is made by batteries, and dynamos that make DC current can only make enough power for small areas. There were now large companies based in Berlin building big generators that made AC power. AC stands for alternating current. Generators that made AC electricity could produce vast amounts of power—enough to light a whole city.

Hermann and Jacob believed the loyal people of Munich would rather buy equipment from a local supplier such as their company. Pauline didn't want to base the family's whole future on this hope. She felt that, loyalty or not, the big power companies might convince the people that one large power plant, far out of town, is better than a bunch of little plants all over town. These were not happy thoughts, and Pauline didn't dwell on them since Hermann and Jacob were so happy about the success of their equipment at the Oktoberfest. But even Albert and little Maja sensed that a dark cloud now hung over the family.

CHAPTER THREE

Learning in Spite of School

The exciting times Albert spent watching and helping his father and Uncle Jacob at the fairgrounds and in the shop only made school seem that much more monotonous. There was one class he liked, though, and that was his religion class.

Most children were exposed to the same religion all of their young lives. But Albert's religious training was more like a banquet. He had a lot to choose from. Albert's mother and father both belonged to the Jewish religion. However, they were both what was known as "freethinking" Jews. They did not practice their faith, and they kept their minds open to the beliefs of other religions. It is not surprising, then, that Albert's parents sent him to a Catholic elementary school. Most of the people of Munich were Catholic, and Albert's parents saw no reason to isolate him from the other children in the city just because he was born into a different religion. They also thought that exposure to another faith would do Albert good, because it would make him more tolerant of people who thought differently than he did.

Albert himself was very religious in a certain way.

He felt that the beauty and mystery of nature, seen in things like magnetism and starry nights, were an expression of the grace of God, and that they were God's work. Therefore, Albert was always keenly interested in hearing what people had to say about God—no matter what label they put on their particular religion—since he so admired and loved God's work.

Though Albert enjoyed his religious instruction at school, it wasn't always for the best. One day, the teacher brought a long, rusty nail to class. The teacher told the class that it was one of the nails that the Jews had used to nail Christ to the cross on which he was brutally slain so many centuries before.

When the other children in Albert's class heard that, they may have been horrified and shocked. They may have stared at Albert and thought, "Jews must be horrible people. How could they do such a thing? If Albert is a Jew, he must be horrible, too." They may have thought all of these things. If they did, Albert didn't notice. He was too good natured for that. As a child, he could not believe that people would ever think badly of him, or of anyone, just because he was of a different religion. That would be far too trivial even to think about.

If the children *had* thought all of those terrible things, it would not have been surprising. Many people in Germany at that time thought badly of Jewish people. They thought they were different from other people, and evil. Such feelings about Jews are called anti-Semitic, and there was a good deal of anti-Semitism in Germany when Albert was a child. The children often learned such hateful feelings from their parents or teachers.

Anti-Semites in Germany used to blame the Jews for everything that went wrong. Jews were said to possess all of the worst character traits. They were said to be greedy and dishonest in business. Many cruel people even claimed that the Jews had been cursed by God, and that they were a lower order of human being.

Albert said later in life that he hadn't noticed any anti-Semitism in Germany until he was a grown man. So it is unlikely that his fellow students paid any attention to their teacher's remarks about the nail. Perhaps the students realized how foolish those remarks were.

In any case, Albert's parents were happy when he went to a new, nonreligious school when he was ten years old. They had had enough of the hurtful way his teachers treated their son. They felt that a new start in a new school might be just the thing for Albert. After all, even though he was shy and had a hard time making friends and getting along with his teachers, he was always a good student. He got very good grades. When it came to arithmetic and mathematics Albert's marks were exceptional. Albert's mother often said that he would surely grow up to be a professor some day. Albert turned this over in his mind. "*Professor* Einstein," he thought, "I like the sound of that."

As things worked out, the teachers in Albert's new school, the Leitpold school, weren't much easier to get along with than those in the old school. They still taught the same dry-as-dust lessons, and they still led their classes in sing-song drills that made one despise, rather than love, the pursuit of knowledge. Albert used to call the teachers in his old school "sergeants" because they loved to run the students through military-like drills. He referred to his new teachers as "lieutenants." They had improved in rank, but not by much.

Albert was far too curious about things to let his schooling hamper his education. He had long ago acquired the habit of thinking for himself. His parents always encouraged him to ask questions about things he didn't understand. As he grew older, Albert got into the habit of reading beyond the books that he was assigned to read in school. His reading opened up a vast new range of ideas to him that he would never tire of exploring.

When Albert had a question concerning mathematics, which wasn't very often, he would usually bring it to his uncle Jacob. Jacob was a brilliant inventor and something of a whiz with math. He would explain mathematical ideas to Albert that the boy would not study in school for many years. Jacob was surprised to find how eagerly Albert listened and how readily he grasped difficult ideas. Often, he would give Albert a hard problem to work on, just so he could get back to his blueprints for a while. He was usually amazed at how quickly and easily Albert would solve the problem. Uncle Jacob also remarked that when Albert solved a mathematical problem, the boy "experienced a deep feeling of happiness." In fact, mathematics was slowly becoming one of the main joys of Albert's life.

There were also people outside the family from

Albert with Uncle Jacob, studying mathematics.

whom Albert learned a great deal. One of those was a young medical student named Max Talmey. In those days, it was a custom in Germany for well-to-do families like the Einsteins to have a student over to their house for dinner once or twice a week. This was done to help poor students get through school. The student that the Einsteins helped in this way was Max Talmey. Max was a tall, slender, well-mannered young man, with a very healthy appetite.

When Max sat down at the Einsteins' table he was hungry for some good home cooking. Albert had a different appetite. He hungered for a glimpse of life in the university, where ideas and concepts nourished the mind and soul.

When Max met Albert he was impressed with the light in the boy's eye and with Albert's quickness and intelligence. He also noticed that Albert's curiosity ran deep. The boy never seemed to run out of questions. When a question was answered, he never forgot the answer, but often thought of a new question that was even more difficult to answer. After a while, Max would arrive at the Einstein house laden with an armful of books for young Albert. Some of these books were to have a deep impact on the boy's quickly developing mind.

At first, Max brought Albert books on all types of science: geology, which is the study of the formation of the earth; and chemistry, the study of the elements of the physical world and how they combine to form different gases, minerals, and metals. He also brought books on physics, which is the study of the physical universe itself—the stars and planets, atoms and molecules, electricity, magnetism, and the laws that govern motion and rest. Albert was absorbed by all of these subjects, but he especially liked physics, which is not surprising. His father and uncle were involved with physics every day in their electronics shop, and Albert himself had long been interested in magnetism and in the stars and planets.

The books that Max brought fueled the lamp of knowledge in Albert's mind until it began to burn brightly. They opened whole new worlds to the boy's inquisitive gaze. They made him think deeply about things that few children think about at such a young age. For one thing, they made him doubt some of the things that he had read in the Bible about the nature of the physical world and how it came to be.

Albert began to believe that some of the explanations

in the Bible about the origins of the universe could not be taken literally. He sought other explanations for these things. Although the books that Max Talmey gave Albert made him question certain explanations found in the Bible, they didn't shake Albert's faith in God. In fact, they only made his desire to know God grow stronger. Albert believed that the structure of the universe represented the way God thinks. He often said that his mission as a scientist was to learn to "read God's mind."

When Max saw how quickly Albert devoured the books he brought, he decided to bring some more difficult books in order to challenge the boy. One day at dinner, when Albert was 13 years old, Max gave him a very difficult book indeed, *The Critique of Pure Reason*, written by a German philosopher named Immanuel Kant. Even its title sounds heavy and ominous. It was decidedly not the sort of book that most thirteen-year-olds read.

Albert, however, was not like most boys his age. He immediately plunged into the difficult book, and found great pleasure reading it. One night, Hermann walked into his son's room to find him fast asleep at his books. Hermann picked up the book that Albert had propped open on his desk. It was *The Critique of Pure Reason*. Hermann looked at the passage that had obviously put his son to sleep. This is what it said:

It can be seen that *time* is the *a priori* formal condition of all appearances whatsoever, whereas space is the *a priori* formal condition of external appearances only. All representations, whether they have or have not external things as their objects, are determinations of the mind. And, as such, they belong to our internal state. Hence they must all be subject to the formal condition of inner sense or intuition, namely *time*.

Hermann closed the book and rubbed his brow. He looked down at Albert, who sat sleeping, his head cradled in his arms atop the desk. For the first time, Hermann thought there was something out of the ordinary about his son. Hermann could understand well enough a child's being a prodigy with mathematics. Hermann himself had been quite a mathematician as a young man. The town of Ulm in Germany, where he and Pauline lived when Albert was born, was known for producing great mathematicians. However, Albert's intellectual gifts went beyond merely being clever with mathematics.

Hermann smiled. "So the Einstein family has produced a philosopher," he thought to himself. He chuckled. Albert probably couldn't understand a word of this difficult tome, he thought to himself. However, he was beginning to feel a bit uneasy about his son, as if there were something about him he would never understand.

Hermann thought that Albert was still a bit too young to grasp what he was reaching for. But Hermann still had to admire his bright young son. Now, more than ever before, Hermann thought that Albert's teachers were fools. How could they possibly be so blind to the value of the boy's curious, eager, penetrating mind—a mind that was so ready to take on new and difficult challenges?

As it turned out, Hermann was wrong about how

31

much of this difficult book, and others like it, young Albert was able to comprehend. But Max Talmey understood. He brought Albert more and more challenging books. After a while, Max admitted that young Albert had gotten even farther into them than he had.

While Albert was rapidly progressing in his private studies, the family business was just as quickly declining. Just as Pauline Einstein had feared, the big power companies had begun to move toward Munich. They promised to build a large power plant outside of the city that would give Munich enough AC power for everyone. People might no longer see the need for the Einsteins' smaller, weaker, DC equipment. The Einsteins might have to look for new ways to make their living.

The family's only hope was uncle Jacob. If only he could come up with another new invention, perhaps their business in Munich could be saved.

Uncle Jacob tried his best. He designed a new device that they could sell to electric power companies. It was an ammeter. Electric current is measured in units called amperes. Uncle Jacob's device was an instrument for measuring the amount of current. It also included a clock. By knowing how much current each customer was using, and for how long, the electric company could compute their bills. Such devices were in great demand in those days when the use of electricity was spreading very fast. If Jacob's ammeter design became popular, the Einstein family might make its fortune yet.

Albert fiddling with ammeter.

When Uncle Jacob showed the new ammeter to his family, young Albert was not thinking of how rich it might make them. He found the device curious for other reasons.

The meter was a large box with a coiled wire attached at the top. Two clocks were fixed to the front of the box. One of the clocks was for recording the time of day. The other clock was for keeping track of the use of electricity. It changed its speed depending on how much current was flowing through the meter at any given time.

Albert thought that these two clocks—measuring two different systems of *time*—were fascinating. He had read, in his difficult book by Kant, that in a certain sense time doesn't exist in the real world but only in the minds of men. Now, here, in Uncle Jacob's device, was a curious use of time. On this strange machine, there was not one precise time, but two very different ones, one of which could change.

As Hermann gaily slapped Uncle Jacob on the back and congratulated him on his marvelous new invention, Albert sat quietly, his head in his hands, and pondered. "This thing called time," he thought, "is very perplexing, indeed."

CHAPTER FOUR

Alone

Max Talmey was amazed at the way Albert devoured the books he brought him. It was as if a much older mind dwelled within the boy. Never jealous or resentful of Albert's quick intelligence, Max continued to bring the lad books.

When Albert was only eleven, Max had given him a textbook on geometry—the mathematical study of measurements in space, of lines, angles, circles and planes. To Albert, the geometry book was special. He called it "the holy geometry book." Albert worked through the entire book by himself, with love of mathematics as his only teacher, while the children in Albert's class at school were still limping through their basic arithmetic.

Since Albert had shown such an ability for mathematics, Max brought him some even more difficult books. These books were on what is called "higher" mathematics, and they were meant for students in the university. Again, Albert tackled them alone. This time he had no choice, for neither Max nor Uncle Jacob knew enough about higher mathematics to help him. According to Max, "The flight of his mathematical genius was so high that I could no longer follow." From now on,

Max would limit his discussions with his young friend to philosophy.

When Albert's education was soaring to new heights, Uncle Jacob's efforts to save the family business were going nowhere. Uncle Jacob entered his new amp-meter in competition at the annual electrical equipment fair. One reviewer said it was "ingenious." Though the machine was much admired, a scientist from Berlin walked off with the prize for his own ammeter design.

To make matters worse, the Einsteins' business in Munich, which had been steady for years, was slowing down. Now the big power companies were threatening to take away what little they had left. But the Einstein brothers did not lose heart. Since business was not good in Munich, they decided to open an electrical equipment shop in Italy, where the people had a great appetite for new electric devices. During the years when they were expanding their operations in Italy, Hermann and Jacob spent a great deal of time away from home, watching over their investments and looking for new customers. When Albert was fourteen years old, there were times when he didn't see much of his father and his uncle Jacob. During these lonely times Albert missed them very much. Memories of their buoyant laughter and lively conversations echoed through the Einstein household, making it seem vast and empty.

Once, while Hermann and Uncle Jacob were away, the rest of the Einsteins had a visitor. It was Cesar Koch, Albert's uncle on his mother's side of the family. Uncle Cesar was a man of high spirits and good humor, and his visits had always been welcome. With the men of the house gone, his arrival was like a breath of fresh air.

Uncle Cesar was a businessman in Antwerp, Belgium. His affairs took him all over Europe and even to America. When Uncle Cesar paid a visit, his baggage was always full of presents that he had gathered in his far-off travels. Best of all, as he unpacked each present, he would also unpack a tale of adventure to go along with it.

Once, when Albert was a small child, his uncle Cesar had brought him a marvelous gift—a model of a steam engine. At that time, steam engines were very important. They powered ships and trains and dynamos and even automobiles. Their workings were simple; they were powered by steam, which was made by heating water with burning coal.

Albert thought that his model was the most amazing gift anyone had ever gotten, and he built it the same day in his father's shop. When he was finished, Uncle Cesar and Uncle Jacob had a long discussion with Albert about how a steam engine works.

Albert would remember the gift of the steam engine all his life. When he was a grown man of thirty he could still draw it from memory. Albert remembered the gift so well because it was from Uncle Cesar, who was always very kind to him and listened closely to what the boy had to say.

Whenever Uncle Cesar came, he would always ask Albert what he had been thinking about lately. He had a feeling that Albert had something very special going on in that inquisitive mind of his. He felt that someday Albert would discover something great, and he turned out to be quite right.

On this latest visit, Albert and his uncle sat in a pair of wingback chairs in the study after dinner and had a long chat. Uncle Cesar told stories of the great Antwerp Bourse, a stock market where men made and lost fortunes within minutes. Uncle Cesar had known men who were tycoons at breakfast and paupers by the time the lunch whistle sounded.

Albert liked to hear these stories, but he never acquired a taste for the world of the marketplace. It always seemed degrading, to be among so many greedy men all the time. Albert preferred to keep to himself and to think. He was convinced that the treasures he would find in his thoughts would make him much richer, and in a way that had nothing to do with money.

When Uncle Cesar got around to asking Albert what was on *his* mind, Albert had plenty to say as well. Albert had been thinking a great deal lately—about light.

Ever since Albert had begun to read books on physics, he had been fascinated by light. Physicists had shown in many experiments that light travels through space as a wave. In many ways, it was like a sound wave. Albert told his uncle that he tried to imagine himself chasing after a beam of light. He tried to imagine what the wave would look like if he could catch up with it.

Uncle Cesar listened very closely, as he always did. He was amused, and at the same time amazed that his young nephew should be considering a problem of this kind so gravely. Other boys his age were still out playing

Chasing beam of light through space.

childish games! Uncle Cesar smiled his great, toothy smile and said, "You must keep me informed of your chase, for if you should ever catch up with this slippery beam of light, I should like to know."

When Hermann and Jacob returned from their latest journey, they were greeted by bad news. Not only had Jacob's ammeter lost the competition at the electrical equipment fair, but it was also selling very poorly. Another device, invented by a scientist who worked for one of the big electric companies, had cornered the market. To make matters worse, the rest of the Einsteins' Munich business had virtually dried up. Something had to be done.

At the dinner table that Sunday, Hermann made an announcement. In a solemn voice, he told the family that the Einstein brothers' electrical equipment shop was

going to move, lock, stock, and barrel, to Milan, Italy.
It was time to unify their business and their family. No
more long separations. The Einsteins would be together
again, in a new country where opportunities abounded.

Hermann had tried to sound hopeful, but the whole
family sensed the disappointment in his voice. He loved
his home and his friends in Munich, and he would never
have thought of leaving if the business were not doing
so badly.

Though Albert was saddened for his father, he was
also glad in a way. He had never liked his school. Indeed,
Germany itself, with all of its military ways, never felt
quite like home to him. It was only for his family that
he felt any real loyalty. They would still be with him in
Italy, a new country full of sunshine and warm, friendly
people. Albert had heard a great deal about the country
from his father and other relatives. He was sure that he
would like living there very much.

But it was not to be.

After Hermann made his announcement, his expression turned grave. He looked at Albert and said sadly,
"The Einsteins will be *almost* all together. You, Albert,
shall remain here to complete your schooling at Leitpold.
I would not wish to disturb your studies. They are too
important to you and to us all. Someday you will make
a fine engineer, but only if you complete your schooling."

Albert's jaw dropped when he heard this. He was
stunned. He could not imagine life in this city without
his beloved family, with whom he had shared so much

over the years. But if his father wished it so, it could be no other way.

On the day his family left Munich, Albert accompanied them to the train station. Albert noticed many soldiers there, arriving from and departing to the distant corners of the country. Albert wondered why there always seemed to be more soldiers at train stations than anywhere else. There were soldiers everywhere in Germany these days. The nation was very proud of the fact that it had more weapons and ammunition, and more good soldiers ready and willing to use them, than any other nation on the globe. Germany was acting like the big bully on the block, shaking its fist and itching for a fight—itching to have its eye blackened, thought Albert.

Albert's eyes were moist with tears as his family waved goodbye from the train. As the train slowly pulled away from the station, its shrill whistle screaming, Albert felt that the mournful whistle echoed his own aching heart.

It was arranged that Albert would rent a small room in the home of some family friends until his education at Leitpold was complete. Though his room was very orderly and clean, with a fine brass bed and a large window that let in lots of daylight, Albert was determined not to like it there. The childless couple that had rented him the room tried to make Albert feel welcome. But nothing seemed to please him. He felt like a baby bird thrown from its nest.

Albert was always a quiet boy, but the glow of his inner cheerfulness had been obvious to anyone. Now, the quiet joy inside him was gone, replaced by something dark and sullen. Before, Albert's teachers had found him to be "difficult" simply because he liked to daydream in their classes. Now, Albert seemed to decide that he would show them what difficult really was.

No longer the dreamer in class, Albert became the cut-up, the clown, the wise guy. He always had something to say to the teacher during lessons, and it was never anything that the teacher wanted to hear. Woe to the teacher if he or she should ever make an error, for Albert's quick mind would pounce on it and show it to the entire class. In this way, Albert could incite gales of laughter in the classroom, but his teacher and the officials of the school were watching him, and they were not laughing.

Albert was not himself at school these days. He felt a pain from an injury deep inside his heart, and the ache grew until it clouded over the kind part of his nature. It made him want to strike back. But when he was alone in his room with only his thoughts, Albert knew that something was wrong.

One night, Albert lay curled up on his bed in his lonely room reading a letter from his family. Albert let his mind wander as he read his father's description of the warm Italian sunshine, the art and architecture in the surrounding towns, and the high green hills and crystal lakes in the peaceful countryside. His father also wrote of the Italian people, who had opened their large hearts to his family. Albert's parents closed the letter, as always, with the wish that he would conclude his studies and join them as soon as he could. Albert decided to take them at their word.

Albert plotted to end his studies immediately, not to wait the long, gray months until graduation. He had decided to flee the dismal Leitpold school. The only question was, how?

The next day, the curtain went up on Act One of a new drama in Munich: Albert Einstein's Nervous Breakdown.

Albert went to pay a visit to his family's doctor. As the frumpy, bearded physician squinted through his monocle at the boy, Albert spun a woeful tale of sleepless nights and tense, nerve-wracked days, of headaches and eye sore, of sweaty palms and anxious thoughts. Albert may have felt a little less guilty by remembering that he had actually had some of these symptoms since his family left town. The rest were the harvest of his fertile imagination.

Albert's doctor had known the Einstein family for years, and he could not believe that this normally shy young man could be faking all of this. He agreed to write a note to Albert's school, asking that he be excused to recover from his apparent nervous collapse. The doctor's prescription for Albert was a trip to Italy to rejoin his family.

This cure took effect fast. Albert skipped away from the doctor's office and almost flew to see the principal at Leitpold. However, his smile dissolved when the principal, after reading the note, informed him that the school had already decided to ask him to leave. They saw no

Expelled from school.

other way to rid their orderly rooms of his obnoxious outbursts. Albert's medical excuse was wholly unnecessary. He was being expelled from school.

Being expelled took some of the fun out of Albert's charade. He hung his head as he stepped through the doors of the school for the last time. But his feelings of hurt and rejection didn't last long. Soon, memories returned of all the injustices he had suffered there—the boring, mindless lessons; the harsh, cruel, small-minded teachers. He would never forget their intolerance for someone who was not cut from the same cloth as other, "normal" children. Albert remembered all of these things, and he felt lucky to have escaped as easily as he had.

The rest of Albert's life in Munich was a blur. He moved like a whirlwind, saying his goodbyes and buying his tickets and packing his life in a rucksack. He wrote to his parents. They were overjoyed at his coming, of course, even if they were a little concerned at the cause.

On a bright, sunny day in the spring of 1895, when Albert was sixteen years old, he said his last goodbyes and was off to the train station. On his last stroll through the streets of Munich, he felt the weight of his rucksack on his shoulder, but he could feel another weight slipping off. It was the weight of his teachers' small-minded concerns, and of his country's desire for war and violence. He was now free of all that.

Albert looked ahead at the smoke pouring from the stack of his approaching train. He could almost see a new life spreading out before him.

CHAPTER FIVE

The Laboratory of the Mind

Albert's family was becoming a regular band of gypsies. Shortly after the Einsteins moved to Milan, they packed their bags once again and relocated in the quiet valley village of Pavia. It was here that their rebellious sixteen-year-old son Albert rejoined them, after the Leitpold school had expelled him.

Pavia was a friendly little farming village tucked in a pleasant countryside of rolling hills and crystal lakes. Here the noise, rush and worries of city life were no more than faraway rumors. There were very few machines—and no soldiers—to disturb the blissful, sublime peace of this place. The local noises were the voices of nature itself—the lowing of cows, the bleating of sheep, and the neighing of horses that pulled wagons along the dusty country roads.

Albert loved to take long walks in the quiet, green hills. Here, away from the narrow-minded teachers and the war-hungry soldiers of Germany, his wandering, curious spirit found room to expand.

One day, Albert and Maja walked to the top of a nearby hill. There, they explored the grounds of a cen-

In Italy with sister, looking at lake and village.

turies-old monastery. They sat atop the chapel steps and looked at the sprawling valley below. They could see the cluster of houses in their little village. A little further beyond lay one of the many lakes of the region, placid and serene, mirroring the blinding noonday sun.

Albert thought about how far the light from the sun had traveled to reach the great unblinking eye of the lake's surface. The sun is about 93 million miles from Earth. Sunlight, traveling at 186,000 miles per second, which is the speed of light, reaches the earth in about eight minutes. Not a very long trip. It took Albert an entire day on the train to travel the 200 miles from Munich to Pavia.

Albert was still spending a great deal of his time puzzling about light, and about many other curious physical phenomena. He felt that if he worked long enough in the quiet laboratory of his mind, he might one day be able to contribute something to the study of physical phenomena.

When such thoughts buzzed in the beehive of Albert's mind, he did not share them, not even with his beloved sister Maja, who sat next to him on the steps of the chapel. They were his private domain and treasure.

Maja looked out over the sprawling valley as she talked to her brother. She told him about the family's life in Italy. If she noticed that Albert's mind sometimes wandered off, she didn't let it bother her. She was used to it. Maja admired her big brother and had great patience where he was concerned. She felt that if she had a mind like his, she would probably let it wander, too.

Albert and Maja strolled lazily back to the village, talking and laughing. Albert noticed how much older his sister seemed. She was just fourteen but she had lately shed a lot of her girlishness. There was now an air of seriousness about her, and she had the dignity that their mother had always possessed. Maja payed little attention to the groups of barefoot Italian boys who followed her with their smiling brown eyes as she walked through the village. She didn't yet notice that she was becoming a comely young woman.

Albert, too, was growing older, becoming more a man and less a child. Perhaps that is why his parents and his uncle were beginning to lose patience with him. They seemed to feel that this handsome, quick-witted young man could begin to take more responsibility on his broad shoulders. Hermann, who once thought Albert something of a nuisance around the shop, now encouraged his son to learn the family trade. He invited Albert to begin to play an active role in the business. Perhaps Albert would like to sit at his uncle's side and learn something of the inventing side of the business. Or he could help Hermann go over the receipts and account books, and learn something of the world of commerce that every man must enter.

Albert did these things to keep the peace in his family, but his heart was not in them. The electrical equipment business had shed the romance and excitement it had held for him as a boy. There was a time when Albert had been thrilled to be in his father's shop, to watch Uncle Jacob build, with his own hands, a working dynamo that would produce huge amounts of power. Now, he realized it wasn't the dynamo he was fascinated with, but the great force of nature that it represented—electromagnetic power. Dynamos produced electricity through the rapid motion of magnets. Though electricians understood that electricity was created in this way, they cared little about *how* or *why* this mysterious power was created. But that was precisely what Albert longed to understand.

Now that Albert was older, he began to study the ideas of the theorists who had made the generation of electric power possible. He studied the works of two great British scientists, Michael Faraday and James Clerk Maxwell. Faraday had done thousands of experiments with electricity and magnetism, and had invented the idea of electric and magnetic fields to explain his results. The rapidly growing electric industry, including the Einstein family business, was based on Faraday's discoveries. But Albert was more interested in fundamental theories. Maxwell had invented a mathematical theory of electricity and magnetism, based on Faraday's work. According to this theory, there might be such a thing as electromagnetic waves, traveling through space at the speed of light. It seemed certain that light waves were a kind of electromagnetic wave.

Maxwell's theory of electromagnetism is generally studied only by advanced students of physics, but Albert had mastered it by the time he was sixteen years old. He used it to try to answer his old question: What would light waves look like if he could catch up with them, and travel along with the waves? It is possible to do this mathematically with water waves, or with sound waves. Albert did the mathematics, and found that the theory of electromagnetism gave him no answer to the question. He could not guess that the answer he found ten years later would revolutionize physics and give the world a new view of the universe.

When Albert Einstein was a young man, electromagnetic phenomena were causing something of a stir in the world of physics. Physical laws that had seemed long settled were suddenly in doubt.

Though there is some dispute about the matter, many people date the beginning of modern physical science from the work of Galileo Galilei, born in Florence, Italy, in 1564. Galileo said that the truth of a physical law can only be determined by experiment. Before his time, many laws were arrived at by logic alone.

Using logic, the ancient Greeks arrived at several apparently logical, though erroneous, laws of motion. They argued, for instance, that a heavier object would fall to the ground faster than a lighter object. This reflected their experience, since a brick certainly fell much faster than a feather when dropped from the same height. Galileo analyzed the problem carefully, and came to the conclusion that the only reason the feather falls so slowly is that the air holds it back. If there were no air, he said, all objects would fall together. Later, when the vacuum pump was invented, the experiment could be tried in a chamber without air. Galileo was proved to be right.

The Greeks also claimed that to keep a body moving, a constant push or pull must be exerted on it. Galileo said that this was not so. A body in motion, said Galileo, would continue in motion until a force is exerted on it to stop it. Newton later called this force *inertia*. A cart that is being pushed along a road does not stop rolling because the force pushing it is removed, but because of the friction between the ground and the wheels. If the friction were removed, the cart would roll on indefinitely, until some other force stopped it.

Galileo was also the first to suggest the notion of the *relativity* of motion. He said that it makes no sense to talk about the motion of an object unless one has some other frame of reference in relation to which the object moves. For example, if you were traveling in a windowless train which is moving at a constant rate of speed, you would not know you were moving at all. But if you could look outside, you would see the trees hurtling by. They provide you with something to compare your motion to; the trees are your frame of reference.

Isaac Newton was born in 1642, the year that Galileo died. In 1687, Newton published a now famous book, *The Mathematical Principles of Natural Philosophy*, which formed the foundation of modern physical science. Newton adopted Galileo's ideas, added some of his own, and provided mathematical explanations for them all. The result was that for the first time scientists had a comprehensive theory of the behavior of the physical universe.

Newton's theories were written in the form of several basic laws which govern the way the universe behaves. One of these, the law of gravity, said that every object in the universe exerts a gravitational "pull" on every other object. Things with large mass, like the stars and planets, pull with more gravitational force than do small things. It is the force of gravity that holds the earth and the sun together and holds things down to the earth. It keeps the planets in their orbits around the sun and the moon in its orbit around the earth.

Newton's mathematical calculations proved to be extremely accurate for predicting the movements of the planets. They also worked well in accounting for the paths of comets, the fall of meteors, and the rise and fall of the tides in the ocean. They are still being used to calculate the paths of artificial satellites. With the development of Newton's theories, men felt they were beginning to understand the mysteries of the universe. Newton, with the help of Galileo and others, had conceived of an orderly universe that behaved like a machine—like clockwork. The collection of Newton's laws eventually became known as "Newtonian mechanics." These are the laws of physics that explain the machine we call the universe.

Newton's mechanics was considered the furthest advance man had yet made on the long road of scientific discovery. They gave men a powerful sense of mastery over the mysterious ways of the universe.

But at the close of the nineteenth century, in the era of electricity, scientists began peering at the tiny, high-speed world of the electron and electric currents, and discovered that some of Newton's esteemed laws were being broken.

Newton had formulated a law called the conservation of mass. This law stated that a particle of matter would tend to stay the same—that is, it would retain its "mass." Now, electrons traveling in a cathode ray near the speed of light were mocking Newton. Their mass did not stay the same, but increased by a hundred or even a thousand times.

Also, in the early part of the nineteenth century, scientists had determined that light was made up of electromagnetic waves of energy, not particles of matter. They had also discovered that magnetism and electricity were two aspects of the same force, electromagnetism. When their research suggested that there might be such a thing as electromagnetic waves, traveling in space at the speed of light, they concluded that light is an electromagnetic wave.

Scientists of the nineteenth century knew about several kinds of waves. They knew that all of them needed some kind of medium to carry them. Water waves, for example, travel through water, and sound waves travel through air. These waves are vibrations of physical objects, gases or liquids. Newton's laws explained them fully. It was natural to suppose that electromagnetic waves also needed a medium to travel through. Thus, scientists invented such a medium, which they called "ether." What the scientists of the day overlooked, however, was that Newton's laws said nothing at all about electricity and magnetism. Just because sound waves need a medium does not mean that light waves do also.

In 1881, Albert Michelson and E. W. Morley set out to measure the speed of the earth through the ether. They used a light beam that was split into two parts. One part traveled in the direction the earth was moving, and was then reflected back by a mirror. The other part traveled back and forth at right angles to the earth's path. They expected to find that the times for the two trips were different. They knew that a boat traveling up a river and back down takes longer to make the trip than a boat traveling the same distance across the river and back. If light was traveling in "ether," there should be a time difference between the two paths.

Michelson and Morley conducted their elaborate experiment time and again. Their instruments were ingenious, and extremely precise, yet they found no difference in the speed of the two beams of light. They were baffled. Newtonian mechanics seemed to require that something like the ether should exist to conduct light through space. However, it could not be detected by experiment. Where was the ether?

Newton's mechanics, his fabulous clockwork theory of the heavens, was in need of repair. It still accurately predicted the actions of the comets and planets. But now, modern experiments, plus a glimpse into the super-high-speed world of electrons and light, had revealed a whole other universe where Newton's laws were not on the books.

Albert knew that if the genius of a giant like Isaac Newton was being questioned, then something very exciting was brewing in the world of physical science. He wanted very much to be a part of that world, to live the life of a thinker and scientist. He even dared to hope that perhaps one day he might offer solutions to the seemingly unanswerable questions that now puzzled scientists.

Albert did not share his new ambitions with his parents. He knew that it was not his place just now to have such grand dreams—at least, not out loud. It was not the place of a high school dropout, with no job and no prospects, and no ambition to succeed in business. He must first finish his education and prove that he had what it takes to be a scientist.

Hermann had hatched a plan. He wanted Albert to travel to the technical university in nearby Zurich, Switzerland, known as the Federal Institute of Technology, to take the entrance exam. There, Albert could learn to become an engineer. He could learn his family's trade and take his place in the family business. Albert liked this plan, for the Zurich University was one of the most distinguished research centers in the world for physics. Once there, he could easily arrange his studies so that he would become not an engineer, as his father wished, but a theoretical physicist.

Albert felt bad about taking the money from his father to make the trip to Zurich. Business in Italy was not as profitable as Hermann and Jacob had hoped. The big electric companies had come here, too. The Einstein brothers had to take out loan after loan just to stay in business. It was a big gamble. There was no telling when they would turn a profit again, if ever. They felt that to compete with the bigger companies, they had to get bigger themselves, and that took money. Hermann had even put the Einstein family's house in Munich up for sale to raise cash.

Albert felt guilty and saddened to hear this. He felt that he was a drain on the family—a sponge that took in but never gave back. He also understood how desperate his father must be to sell the family's beloved house in Munich. It was as if their moorings were suddenly cut, and they were now drifting, unsure of where they would end up in the world. Albert knew how hard it must have been for his father to cut away their roots this way.

In Zurich, the university officials were surprised to see such a young man applying to take their entrance exam. Albert was still only sixteen and the students were normally eighteen years old before they entered the university. However, they agreed that if Albert could pass the test, he would be welcome to study there. As it turned out, that was a big "if."

Albert felt comfortable taking the test. After all, it was in German. He hadn't heard or read much German during his stay in Italy, apart from his own books and his conversations with his family. Albert didn't learn foreign languages easily, and his Italian was never very good. It was refreshing for him to be in a German-speaking country again. That was one of the good things about Switzerland.

There were other things about this country that appealed to Albert. For one thing, the Swiss people were among the most peaceful in the world. They had soldiers, a large army in fact. But they had it for one reason only—to insure that no country would violate their peaceful lifestyle. The Swiss would never start a war to gain new territory as other countries did. They were content with their lives, and with their clean, beautiful country just the way it was.

Albert liked Switzerland, and he had a great deal of respect for the university. It had the best equipment for physics research to be found anywhere in the world. The top students from many nations came here to learn to solve the great riddles of physical research, the same riddles that consumed so much of Albert's thoughts.

But it was not to be. Albert failed his entrance exam at the F.I.T., and not by a hair. He failed every subject miserably, except physics and mathematics. However, he showed an acute grasp of the concepts of higher mathematics and physics. His scores in these subjects were so remarkable that the instructors were impressed with him anyway. They advised Albert to finish high school and return later to the university, at which time they would be proud to enroll him. With a high school diploma, Albert could be admitted to the university without an exam.

The instructors thought Albert should attend high school in the nearby town of Aarau. Albert liked this idea. It meant that he could stay in Switzerland, and he could still please his parents by returning to school.

Albert returned to Pavia and packed his rucksack once again.

CHAPTER SIX

Peace

On a bright morning in October 1895, Hermann accompanied Albert on the train trip to his new school at Aarau. As the train chugged across the valley near the northern border of Italy, the two travelers gaped at the distant, hulking mountains that swung into view. These were the Swiss Alps, inching closer like an army of sluggish giants, their heads hidden in the clouds.

The Alps help make Switzerland the isolated, peace-loving nation that it is. They had provided an almost impenetrable natural barrier to the outside world for centuries. The frosty heights of these mountains were covered with snow and ice the year round. To attempt to cross them with an army of horse and foot soldiers was impossible, though many had tried.

Albert felt that Switzerland was God's country. It was a land protected by nature's mountains from the hot-blooded adventures of men of war. He would welcome the chance to live there. The Swiss, above all, were lovers of peace. They had sworn never to invade another country, and never to join an alliance in war.

Albert thought of Switzerland as a place of quiet. He appreciated the quality of Swiss chocolate as well as Swiss

On train through Alps to Switzerland.

watches. He loved the hills of the Swiss countryside, dappled with pastel-colored spring flowers. He liked the fact that the International Red Cross, an organization of peace and brotherhood, made its home in Switzerland. Albert had decided to make his home in this peaceful country, too. He had even decided to take a very strong step, to swear allegiance to the Swiss republic, and to officially renounce his German citizenship.

During the train ride to Aarau, Albert told his father of his desire. He did not want to be a German citizen when he turned seventeen years old in a few months, for then he would be eligible to be drafted into the German army. The thought of this sickened him. He wished to sever all ties with Germany. The law required that Albert's father give his permission.

Hermann had been staring out the window at the cloud-capped mountains. Now, he seemed to spring awake. "My son," he said, "I admire your idealism, and your love of peace, but do not get romantic about this country. If you thought that Germany had a lot of soldiers, you haven't seen anything."

"The Swiss have one of the strongest armies on Earth," Hermann explained. "Most countries only make their young people serve as soldiers. In Switzerland, all men serve, beginning at the age of twenty, for thirty years. No wonder people say that Switzerland doesn't *have* an army, Switzerland *is* an Army. The Swiss maintain a strong army to discourage anyone from disturbing their peace.

"You see those gentle mountains ahead," Hermann continued. "Many of them have been hollowed out. Some of the most powerful guns in Europe are hidden within those mountain caves, ready to explode in a firestorm if an army were to invade this nation. Why, some of the mountain caves are large enough to hold an entire regiment of Swiss soldiers. The Swiss are some of the best soldiers in the world. Napoleon himself, the great world conqueror, said that."

Albert knew that this was true about the Swiss. They were the most skilled mountain climbers and skiers in the world. This nation of gifted watchmakers also had many crack rifle shots and crafty demolitions experts. They were not a people to take lightly.

Albert thought it strange that these people had to be so good at war in order to live their lives in peace. They were like the shy porcupine. Attack it, and it will roll up in a ball and stick out its sharp quills.

Hermann and Albert rode the train all the way to Zurich, where they took a room for the night at a pension, a very small, quaint hotel. The next morning they went to the immigration office. Albert gravely filled out the citizenship papers, putting it in black and white that he no longer wished to be considered a German. Then the official held out a Bible. Albert put his right hand on the Bible and swore an oath of allegiance to Switzerland. Hermann watched the scene. He could not help but feel proud of Albert, even though he thought his action was a bit extreme.

But it was very important to Albert to renounce his German citizenship. He had always hated the Germans' rigid, militaristic ways, and lately, things had gotten even more serious. German writers and thinkers had begun to say that Germans were created by nature as superior beings, better than any other people in the world. It was only natural, according to this logic, that the Germans should rule the world. Some writers even said that people should be bred like animals to insure that inferior breeds died out and that only the best—the Germans—would survive.

Albert saw the madness in these ideas that were beginning to take hold in his country. He would not allow anyone to call him a son of such a nation. But the papers for his Swiss citizenship would not go through for years yet, so for now Albert was the son of no nation. He was an alien in a new land, and he liked it that way.

Albert bade his father farewell at the Zurich train station. He traveled alone to the village of Aarau.

The high school in Aarau was not the sort of place that Albert had expected. He was pleasantly surprised. He had always known schools to be nasty, boring places. This school was a friendly place. The teachers were outgoing and warm. They were even *fair* in their dealings with students. Albert was younger than any of the other students in his class, but he was not treated any differently because of this, either by students or teachers. Albert could scarcely believe that he was on the same planet.

At Aarau, the classes were organized by subject matter. Albert went to one room to study mathematics, and to another room to study literature, and there was a different teacher for each subject. Albert liked this system. He liked the freedom he found here. He also enjoyed his classes. There was nothing of the old German drill-sergeant in these Swiss teachers. They actually seemed to like teaching—and students!

Albert lived in the home of the headmaster of Aarau, Herr Professor Jost Winteler, and his large, friendly family. Herr Winteler was a gentle man of great intelligence, patience and warmth. Albert used to study him—his high domed forehead and mane of graying hair, his sturdy chin, and especially his eyes, bright with intelligence. Albert got a strange feeling when he met this man's deep, gentle gaze. "Here is a man who *sees* me," he thought, "a man who understands me and cares." Albert had never felt this way about a teacher before. If the truth be told, he had always considered himself to be smarter than his teachers, even when he was quite young. "Finally," Albert thought, "I have a teacher worth having."

Professor Winteler was active outside of his teaching at Albert's school. In his spare time, he also did some research work in the field of linguistics, the study of languages. Once, Albert visited Herr Winteler in his study. Albert had come to ask permission to go with his class on a hike in the Alps, but he quickly found himself in a discussion with Herr Winteler about linguistics.

Herr Winteler told Albert about a paper he was writing. It concerned a thing he called the "relativity of languages." Herr Winteler tapped his pipe and refilled it. Then he said, "people with different languages think differently. The people of the Masai tribe in Africa think differently than the Dutch people of Amsterdam, for instance." Albert knitted his brow in puzzlement.

The professor sat back in his chair and lit his pipe. He then explained that, "people living in different places invent different words for things, and then the words control how they think. The Masai people, for instance, do not have a word that means 'the future.' Therefore, when they talk of time, they always talk about the *present* time."

Albert was now fascinated. Here was another example where time, something everyone took for granted, was not an absolute thing, not the same for all people.

Professor Winteler teaching about time and the future.

For him time had always had three dimensions: past, present, and future. "But people with no word for anything but past and present times don't think of time in the same way," he thought. "They don't think of tomorrows, only of yesterdays and today."

"The fact that some people have no idea of future time might lead to interesting things," explained the professor. "Hope, for example, lives in the future," he said. "The things one hopes for are always things in the future. So the Masai people may never have felt hope, since they have no idea of a future."

Albert was spellbound. Herr Winteler smiled a broad, wise smile, and said, "But, if the Masai live without hope, they also live without fear. For fear is always about the future, too." Albert smiled when Herr Winteler said this. He thought it was very clever, indeed.

Later, when Albert's class arrived on the sunny Alpine trail for its hike up the mountain, Albert was still thinking about the things Herr Winteler had said. The class climbed higher and higher, planting their alpenstocks—a long, pointed staff—into the ground to keep their balance. Albert was thinking about his book by Kant, which said that time exists in the mind only. Now, he had learned that ideas of time can be "relative," that is, different for different people, depending on the words they use for talking about it. How wonderful, thought Albert, to have a job that allowed one to speculate about such things, like Herr Winteler. Albert mused on these things as the valley floor got further and further away, and the trees and people below got smaller and smaller.

The next several seconds were a blur. Albert had been daydreaming too much to pay strict attention to this hike up the steep slope of the mountain. He tripped over a sharp crag, and stumbled back toward the edge of a high cliff. As he slipped toward the cliff he could almost see his life being snuffed out on the rocks in the valley far below. Just in time—a splinter of a second before Albert would have fallen to his death—a classmate hooked him around the waist with his alpenstock. The trembling Albert held on to the stick as the rest of the boys pulled him back to safety.

"You must be watchful at these heights, Herr Einstein," said the teacher, who was along as the boys' guide

Slipping while hiking.

on the hike. "What were you thinking about?" he asked. Albert stood and brushed himself off. Then, he answered, "I was wondering what time it is; perhaps I got carried away."

The year Albert spent at Aarau was a happy one. For the first time, Albert liked school, and he became even more fond of physics than he had been before. Albert also became very close to the professor and to his large, friendly family. (Albert's sister Maja would one day unite the Winteler and Einstein families by marrying one of Professor Winteler's sons, a marriage that would be very happy.) At the end of the year, Albert had finally earned his high school diploma, and he was at last ready to enroll at the technical university in Zurich.

The Federal Institute of Technology was also called

the F.I.T., the Swiss Polytechnic, or simply the "Poly." It was one of the foremost schools of technical education in Europe and in all the world. Students came from many nations to receive the latest in technical training in electromagnetic theory, physics and engineering.

The laboratories at F.I.T. were famous and much envied. They contained countless galvanometers, which are used to measure the force of electric currents, and hundreds of batteries, which were much more rare and expensive than they are today. Also available were the most expensive kinds of microscopes then available, three and four to a room.

These laboratories were a joy to Albert. He had always done much of his best work in the laboratory of his own mind, but to become a theoretical physicist he had to master the experimental laboratory as well. This he did earnestly, spending entire days and nights in the laboratory, running experiment after experiment.

Albert was not as eager when it came to attending lectures. He almost never went to them. He found them boring and didn't think he would learn anything useful from them. His physics class, for example, concentrated on ideas that to him seemed covered in cobwebs, such as Newtonian mechanics and the classical aspects of physics. Albert's teacher did not cover the new discoveries in electromagnetism, but these were the ideas that fired the intellect and soul of young Albert.

Instead of boring himself with lectures, Albert spent his time in the solitude of his boarding-house room, reading the latest theories. He was fascinated by the idea that magnetism, electricity and light were all electromagnetic waves that moved at the speed of light. For three years Albert would stay huddled in his den during the day and see almost no one, content to be alone with his books. From time to time, unshaven and sloppily dressed, he would appear in the street to take a meal or perform some errand. Then it was back to his room for more study. At night Albert would make his appearance. He would meet one of his few friends for coffee and a discussion of physics. Or he might go off to the lab, which was now empty of other students and teachers, to test some theory he had read about.

During this time in the university, Albert had few friends, and he was not always friendly to be around. He had patience only for those things that interested him. One teacher summed up the feelings of perhaps all of Albert's teachers when he said, "You know, Einstein, you are a clever enough fellow, but you have one serious fault. You won't listen to anyone."

Albert seemed to think he knew everything. He seldom went to class, but when he did he was often flippant with his teachers. One day, on an outing with a geology class, Albert's teacher asked him which way the strata in the rocks were flowing, up from below, or vice-versa. "It is pretty much the same to me whichever way they run, Professor," was Albert's reply.

While at the F.I.T., Albert met Marcel Grossman, a gentle man who laughed easily, and who was convinced that Albert was a genius. Marcel would remain Albert's friend the rest of his life.

Marcel was as dedicated to his classes as Albert was disinterested in his. Marcel always went to his lectures and took very meticulous notes. That was lucky for Albert. At the end of the four-year university course, each student had to take a comprehensive exam. Albert would surely have failed the exam, since he missed so many classes, without the help of his friend Marcel's notes. For a whole month Albert crammed night and day from these notes. During this time he slept very little, and drank quarts of coffee to stay awake. The experience was not pleasant, but Albert passed his exams and graduated from college.

In those days, however, a college degree was not enough. To get a job, especially as a physics teacher, one needed a recommendation from a professor. Albert, with his reclusive ways, had never really charmed any of his professors. Not one of them was willing to write him a recommendation, though many saw how bright he was. They felt his arrogance overshadowed his obvious ability in physics.

Without a recommendation, Albert could not find a job. His allowance, which had been paid by relatives while he was a university student, was discontinued. Penniless and jobless, Albert was forced to return to Italy and his family. He felt very guilty. He had spent a lot of the family's money during four years of college. Now that he had graduated, what did he have to show for it?

CHAPTER SEVEN

Window to a New Universe

lbert's return to Italy was not a joyous occasion. He had hoped to come home a professor of physics. Instead, he was unemployed, and, except for his degree, which he now saw as a meaningless piece of parchment, Albert felt that he was no different than before.

Albert was ashamed to face his father and his family. The charms of the Italian countryside were gone for him. He could not even find solace in his thoughts of physics, for the ordeal of cramming his head full of outdated concepts for his exams had left a bad taste in his mouth for science. It would be months before he could think of physics with his former joy.

Albert wrote letter after letter to universities seeking an appointment as an assistant professor. He wasn't interested in making a lot of money, just enough to support himself. He did not wish to be a drain on his family any longer. As usual these past few years, the family business was limping along, barely surviving. Albert felt he had to find a job—any job.

After months of unemployment and near despair, a

letter came from Albert's old college friend, Marcel Grossman. Marcel's father knew a man at the Swiss patent office in the city of Bern. He would be willing to recommend Albert for a position that was about to open up, that of an inspector of patents for new inventions. Most of these were electrical inventions, the kind Albert's uncle Jacob had made. Albert was not an engineer, but Marcel's father had heard enough about his son's ingenious friend to feel that Albert was equal to the job.

On hearing this news, Albert was filled with new hope. He soon moved to Bern, even before he got the appointment at the patent office. Once there, he took a part-time job as a mathematics tutor to enable him to survive while he waited for his new job to open up.

A few months later, Albert finally began his new duties at the patent office. He was overjoyed at being able to make his own way in the world, finally, at the age of twenty-three. His joy was short-lived, however. A few months after he began work, his father, who had been ill, passed away. Hermann's death greatly saddened the Einstein family. Albert would always remember the sound of his laughter and his generous heart.

Now, it was more important than ever for Albert to make a success of himself. He had his mother and sister to think of. One day soon, they would no longer be able to live on the meager estate that his father had left behind.

Albert wished to become settled in his new life in Bern. He now had a job, but he wanted something more. He wanted companionship.

A few months after his father died, Albert got mar-

Working at patent office.

ried. His new wife's name was Mileva Maritsch. Albert had met her at the university, where Mileva was also a physics student. Mileva was a very beautiful woman. Like Albert's mother, Mileva had an air of dignity and grace about her. She had flowing, dark hair, and her deep brown eyes were full of passion. However, Albert's mother, Pauline, was against his marriage to Mileva. She did not like the fact that Mileva seemed so dark and moody all of the time. She felt her son would prefer someone a bit more cheerful. As usual, Albert listened to nothing but his own heart. He married Mileva, and the couple settled down to live in the peaceful town of Bern.

Life now seemed ordered and secure to Albert. He

had a job and a wife, and soon Mileva would bear him his first son, Hans Albert Einstein. There was a sense of sameness and continuity now to Albert's world, which was the way he wanted it. He had other things to think about, things he had neglected for too long.

Albert had not been able to concentrate on physics for some time after his final exams at the university. Now that he was settled down, he wanted to get back to his old love. His mind was ablaze with new ideas, which he felt might lead him somewhere unexpected and wonderful.

Albert's job was ideal, in a way, for a man of his thoughtful temperament. Every morning he would receive a stack of patent applications. These were usually designs for new electrical devices, the kinds that he had seen so often in the Einstein brothers' shop. Albert was able to easily grasp the essentials of these applications, and could dispose of them hastily. This left him with a lot of free time. Albert used this time to reenter a familiar place, the laboratory of his mind, where he practiced his first love, theoretical physics.

Once Albert cleared his morning's work from his desk, he would sit back and ponder his latest physics problem, often scribbling complicated formulas on scraps of paper. If his boss came by, Albert hid the scraps of paper in a drawer and pretended to get on with the work that he had already finished. His boss never suspected how quickly Albert was able to get things done, so his charade succeeded. If Albert's boss had ever caught on to the sorts of things the young patent inspector was scribbling on those scraps of paper in his desk, he would have turned white with shock.

During those early days at the patent office, Albert's mind was on fire with thoughts about an old and perplexing subject, light. Albert was convinced that he had discovered something important in relation to light, something that also had to do with another perplexing subject, the concept of time. Albert felt that his thoughts would be of interest to physicists the world over.

Later in life, Albert said that his years in Bern were his happiest. He made new friends, people who were also interested in current ideas. Albert and his friends would meet in a cafe during the evening hours for long, spirited discussions. From time to time, Albert would share with his friends some of his new ideas about physics, and they would marvel at the complexity of his thoughts. His energy seemed boundless to them, like that of a man possessed. They were sure that soon their ardent young friend, who spoke with such enthusiasm about physics, would give birth to an amazing theory. Albert himself was not quite sure what that new theory would be, but for the time being, he was content to think—his favorite occupation.

In the year 1905, when Albert was twenty-six years old, he decided that he had done enough thinking for a while. During that year he wrote four papers which he published in the most prestigious physics journal in Germany, *Annalen der Physik*. Some of the ideas in these papers would shock the entire scientific world, and change the way people viewed the universe.

The most important of these papers was titled, "On the Electrodynamics of Moving Bodies." The title is important, for in this paper Albert used the concepts discovered in electromagnetic research to update Newtonian mechanics. Newton had described an orderly, *mechanical* universe that ran like a clock. Now, Albert Einstein, living in Switzerland, the land of watchmakers, dismantled and rebuilt Newton's clock, using high-speed *electrodynamic* principles. The results he got were astonishing, and to many, unbelievable.

Scientists always search for things that are "constant," things that don't change. Constants make it easier to measure things that *do* change.

In his theories, Albert employed a new constant that solved many difficulties. He said that the speed of light is a universal constant. Light always travels at 186,000 miles per second. Even if one were to shine a light from a fast-moving source, one would still get the same answer. Furthermore, Albert said that the speed of light is the highest possible speed that can occur in the universe. It is the universal speed limit.

Galileo had said, and Newton had confirmed, that in a mechanical universe, speeds add up. That is, if one shines a light from a car moving at 60 miles per hour, for example, the speed of the car would be added to the speed of the light and make it faster. However, later experiments showed this idea to be false and Einstein's idea to be true. Light does not obey Newton's law of the addition of velocities—it always moves at the same speed.

This was the first of the gears to be removed from Newton's clock.

Einstein had finally solved his childhood riddle: What would one see if one followed a beam of light as it hurtled through space? The answer is that there is no answer. If you try to follow a beam of light, it is impossible, for nothing can travel as fast as light. You will find that you can never catch it. Even if you are going 180,000 miles a second to chase a beam of light, you will find that it is running away from you at 186,000 miles a second. No matter who is measuring the speed of light, or under what conditions, the answer is always the same.

Einstein had never agreed with Lorenz's explanation for the increase in mass of an electron moving at speeds near the speed of light. Now, he had a better answer. The electron's mass increases at very high speeds because it is approaching the universe's speed limit, and the enormous amounts of energy needed to attain such high speeds actually weigh on the electron to keep it from ever reaching the speed of light.

The concept of mass is like that of weight, but more specifically, mass refers to an object's *resistance* to changes in motion. Einstein showed that the enormous energy needed to make an electron move very fast also makes its mass increase; that is, it makes its resistance to motion greater.

The increase in the mass of the electron seemed to be the action of a kind of universal traffic cop. It enforced the universe's speed limit, the speed of light. The electron needs so much energy to approach the speed of light that it will always take on too much mass and become too "heavy" ever to actually attain that speed.

Einstein had discovered the "relativity" of the measurement of mass. The increase in the mass of an electron at high speeds has nothing to do with the electric charge, as Lorenz had claimed. We see this unusually large mass because we are viewing the electron from a different frame of reference, moving with respect to the electron. If you could ride along with the electron, you would not see it in motion. This is a familiar idea. If you are traveling in a jet plane, for example, the magazine you are holding in your lap is not moving, in your frame of reference. However, if you look out the window, you see the whole world moving backwards. In just the same way, if you are riding a fast-moving electron, it is not in motion with respect to you, and it has the same mass it has at rest. But everything else is moving, and you would find that all other objects in the universe have unusually large masses.

This relative increase in mass applies to all bodies when they speed up. However, it is only *noticeable* when the speed is very high—such as the speed of an electron in a cathode ray, which approaches the speed of light.

To take a hypothetical example, suppose your mass is 50 kilograms. Now suppose you are in a highly unlikely train, moving at 90 percent of the speed of light. If you step on a scale, the scale will still read 50 kilograms because the scale is in your frame of reference. But if someone outside the train, at rest on the earth, were to measure your mass, he would find it to be 115 kilograms. Mass depends on the frame of reference from which it is measured. It is a relative measurement.

As things speed up to nearly the speed of light they take on so much more energy that their mass increases. The discovery of this relationship between mass and energy was a real shock to the world of physics. A rule of physics had been that if one kind of energy disappears, it turns up as another kind. For example, you can add energy to a piece of wood by sandpapering it vigorously: it gets hot. The energy appears in the form of heat. Or you can connect a motor to a battery, thus using up electrical energy to make something move. But in Einstein's analysis of the relativity of mass, something new was happening. Adding energy to an electron did not change anything except its mass. If the rule about energy were true, it must mean that mass is just one more form of energy. This relationship was so puzzling that even Einstein needed a few more months to think about it.

A few months after Einstein published his paper on the special theory of relativity, he published another paper that analyzed the relationship between energy and mass. In this paper he developed a simple mathematical formula that would eventually change the world. It is one of the most famous formulas ever to come out of a physicist's mind: $E = mc^2$. The formula says that energy and mass are just two different aspects of the same thing. All mass is energy, and all energy is mass. A hot potato has more energy than a cold one, and therefore it also has more mass. You could never measure this by putting the potato on a scale because the amount of mass increase is extremely small. If you were to heat a 500-gram potato in the oven to 450 degrees Farenheit, its mass would increase by only five billionths of a gram. Energy only has an obvious effect on mass when large quantities are involved, like the amount of energy required to move something nearly as fast as the speed of light.

Einstein's formula tells us that a tiny amount of mass equals an enormous amount of energy. In the formula $E = mc^2$, E stands for the amount of energy, m for the mass and c for the speed of light. To find the energy equivalent of a given mass, you multiply the speed of light by itself, and then by the mass. Since the speed of light is tremendous—186,000 miles per second—multiplying it by itself and then by the mass, even if the mass is quite small, will result in an enormous amount of energy. If you could convert all the mass of a couple of pounds of coal into electrical energy, it would turn into 25 billion kilowatt-hours of useful electricity. This is as much as is produced in several weeks by all the power plants in the United States. However, our usual methods of converting matter into other forms of energy are much less efficient, for all they can do is convert that coal into ashes and enough heat to barbecue a couple of hamburgers.

Albert's theory of the *equivalence* of matter and energy could not be proven right away, but when it was, the world realized that knowledge of this kind could be very powerful, indeed. The theory was proven in the explosion of atomic bombs, the most powerful weapons ever built. Atomic bombs convert matter to energy very efficiently, though the result is the most horrible weapon ever built, capable of enormous destruction. Observers at the first experimental explosion of an atomic bomb said that the brightness of the blast made it look like a miniature sun. The comparison makes sense, since the sun, like an atomic bomb, also creates its radiant energy in an atomic reaction, though a different sort of reaction than is used in an atomic bomb. Albert's formula explained the process by which the sun and all the other stars in the universe are able to burn so brightly for billions and billions of years. They are very efficient at converting matter to energy.

Albert had shown that some unexpected things were happening to objects traveling at very high speeds in the universe. Things that travel near the speed of light use so much energy that they begin to take on mass. They finally take on so much mass that they can never break the universal speed limit—the speed of light. This additional mass showed the underlying unity of matter and energy—it showed that energy had mass, though it was hard to detect at normal, everyday levels of energy.

Einstein also showed scientists some other curious things they had never noticed about the high-speed universe. These things have to do with *measurements*. Just as high speeds affect the measurement of mass in different frames of reference, so too are other measurements affected by changing the speed of the body being measured or the speed of the observer doing the measuring. These measurements are "relative" to the frame of reference of the observer, hence the title, "special theory of *relativity*."

Einstein's theory expanded Galileo's concept of relativity. Galileo had claimed that motion is relative. Albert expanded this idea to cover measurements. He explained that these, too, are relative—to the frame of reference of the person doing the measuring.

Einstein did not invent relativity. Galileo did, centuries before. He figured out that things in motion, like flying cannonballs or falling stones, obey the same rules in all frames of reference. This means that if you stay within your own laboratory and do not look out, you cannot tell whether the laboratory is at rest or moving at a steady speed. If you have ever been in a jet plane, you know this. As long as the plane is flying steadily, the cabin attendant can pour the coffee in just the same way as if the plane were sitting on the runway. The only way you can tell it is moving is by looking out the window, at another frame of reference—the clouds and the earth below.

Einstein added only one idea to this theory. He assumed that electromagnetic waves, including light, obey the same rule. He might have said, "I can measure the speed of light in a laboratory. If the relativity principle is true, I should get the same answer in a jet plane, whether the plane is moving or not." That is why Michelson and Morley could not detect the motion of the earth by using light beams. The speed of light in their equipment was the same whether or not the apparatus was in motion.

Einstein proposed that the speed of light is a constant and that it is the fastest possible speed. Electromagnetic waves can go that fast, but no material object can. We have already seen the effect on the measurement of the mass of an electron as it approached the speed of light. Einstein showed that other measurements as well were affected when objects moved at such speeds.

Einstein's ideas about the effects of very high speeds on measurements produced results so strange that it took physicists many years to accept them. He found, for example, that as a moving object approaches the speed of light, it shrinks. Imagine, for example, two identical rocket ships, 50 feet long. One is sitting on the ground and the other is flying over it, at 90 percent of the speed of light. Suppose someone on the ground were pointing an instrument at that flying ship to measure its length. The answer he would get is 22 feet. The ship traveling at a speed near that of light has shrunk! The pilot in the rocket ship would not notice the difference, because his meter bar also would have shrunk.

This concept of contraction at high speeds was not new. Lorenz had noticed it. He explained it on the basis of his electron theory. He used it to explain why the Michelson-Morley experiment had failed. What happened, he said, was that their instrument shrunk in the direction of motion. Lorenz even produced a mathematical formula to calculate the amount of contraction.

Einstein took the next logical step. If all motion is relative, he said, then the pilot in the moving rocket ship has a right to consider himself at rest. In the pilot's frame of reference, it is the ship on the ground that is moving—*backwards*. Therefore, if he measures the length of the ship on the ground, he will find that it is only 22 feet long. The law is the same for both pilots: moving objects shrink.

This was more than physicists could swallow. They had to think that if ship A is shorter than ship B, ship B must be longer than ship A. Anything else violates common sense. But which one is *really* shorter? Einstein would answer, "The question is meaningless. It depends on the frame of reference from which you view it. This is the logical answer, no matter what your common sense may say." It took scientists a number of years to come around to this way of thinking.

Michelson and Morley were trying to measure the speed of the earth with respect to the ether. Einstein tells us that this makes no sense. The only way you can measure motion is with respect to some other object. The speed of light has to be measured with respect to some laboratory. There is no ether.

Even stranger, measurements of time are also relativistic. If the pilot of the moving rocket and a friend on the ground were to use their watches to time the same event, they would get different measures. For example, the man on the ground times himself and finds that it takes him 20 seconds to comb his hair. For the pilot watching from above, this is taking place in a moving frame of reference. If he times it with his watch, he will find that it takes his friend 46 seconds to make his hair presentable.

We say that events occur *simultaneously* when they appear to happen at the same time. Imagine that someone

Demonstrating one of Einstein's theories.

is standing in a field, midway between two trees—say an oak and a maple. Lightning strikes both trees. An observer sees it happen and says, "both trees were struck at exactly the same time." The lightning actually struck just a little before he saw it, since the flashes of light had to travel from the trees to his eyes. But if he is exactly midway between the trees, the light would take the same length of time to travel from the oak to his eyes as from the maple. Therefore, in his frame of reference, the two bolts are simultaneous.

Now suppose someone drives by in a very fast car, moving from the oak toward the maple. The car passes the midpoint just as the lightning strikes. By the time the light from the oak tree reaches the car, the car has passed the midpoint, so the light has traveled more than halfway. Since the car is now closer to the maple tree, the light from the maple has traveled less than halfway. Since both flashes of light move at the same speed, the one from the maple tree will get to the car first, so the driver will see one flash before the other. In the driver's moving frame of reference, the events are not simultaneous.

What all this shows is the *relativity* of the measurement of time. This idea shocked scientists, for time was always thought to be a constant, unvarying thing. It was felt to run in a "stream" throughout the universe, and to be the same everywhere. Now Albert had shown that time is *relative* to the motion of the observer. If two observers are stationary, they will measure the same value for time. However, if one observer is moving, and especially if one is moving very rapidly *relative* to another, then the two observers will measure time quite differently.

The most important thing about the measurements made by the two observers, each moving with respect to the other, is that both are *correct* in their own frame of reference. The driver of the car is right when he says that the lightning struck the maple first, and the man standing in the field is right when he says that both trees were hit at the same time. Each is right in his own frame of reference. Now physicists know that when they state measurements of mass, time, length, velocity or other quantities, they must be careful to indicate the frame of reference from which the measurements were made.

Einstein's paper in which he explained all of these curious results is one of the most important writings in the history of science. It altered the most basic ideas of physics. Newton had viewed the universe as a cosmic clock, in which stars and planets were kept in their orderly paths by universal gravity. According to Newton, matter was matter, not "frozen" potential energy; velocities added to velocities equaled greater velocities; measurements of time and length were the same for everyone. Newton's laws are still valid in the everyday world of slow-speed phenomena in which we live. But Albert Einstein's theory opened a window on another aspect of the universe. It showed the complex and often bizarre results of super-high-speed motion in the universe. Such speeds take place in the miniscule world of the atom, and in the expansive world of the stars, planets and galaxies that hurtle through space. These speeds show us that measurements of time, space and mass are *relative* to the person doing the measuring; they make energy take on massive proportions; and they show us a velocity—the speed of light—that remains the same constantly and cannot be added up with other velocities to become greater.

Newton's universe was a clock, set in motion by God and allowed to run by itself. It was based on three firm and rigid gears: absolute time, which was the same all over the universe; space, where every object had its own rigid size and position; mass, which did not change. Einstein showed that the gears are flexible. His clock obeys a different set of rules. Scientists following Newton had invented the ether as a framework for space. To them, an object was "at rest" when it was not moving with respect to the ether. In many experiments, they were unable to find out exactly what kinds of properties this ether had. Einstein solved the problem by getting rid of the ether altogether. There is no framework in space, he said. There is no such thing as being "at rest" in the universe. All motion is relative. Scientists had also claimed that the ether must exist for it is needed to conduct light waves through space. Einstein said that electromagnetic waves need no medium in which to travel.

In 1905, one issue of *Annalen der Physik* contained three papers by the unknown inspector in the Swiss patent office, Albert Einstein. Any one of them would have made his reputation as a great theoretical physicist. The first, for which he was awarded the Nobel prize in 1921, was about the photoelectric effect. When light strikes a metal, it may knock electrons off the surface of the metal. To explain this effect, Einstein had to assume that light comes in tiny energy packets. Each little packet knocks out one electron. Light, he said, has two kinds of properties: it is both wave and particle. Einstein called particles of light *photons*, from the greek word "photo," which means light. Einstein's explanation was so outrageous that few physicists could accept it. A few years later, they had to. There was just no other way to explain the results of experiments on the photoelectric effect.

The second paper presented a mathematical theory

of the motion of molecules. Chemists and physicists of the day knew about molecules. Einstein's paper gave additional proof that they exist, and suggested an experiment to find out how big they are. The experiment was done a few years later.

The third paper was the famous one on relativity. This one and the paper on photons were revolutionary. They told physicists that some of their most fundamental ideas were wrong. Ever since Newton, physicists had assumed that space, time and mass are rigidly fixed. When Einstein told them that they are not, many people felt that he was being illogical. The truth is the exact opposite. His method was to apply rigid logic to the results of experiments, no matter where they led. He was ready to accept any logical outcome, no matter how outrageous. This special ability made Albert Einstein the greatest physicist since Newton. Relativity and the photon theory were triumphs of logic over common sense.

While Albert sat in his cozy living room and read the copy of the physics journal in which his three papers were printed, he felt a great sense of accomplishment. He realized that his ideas were revolutionary. He only wondered if the great scientists of the world would accept them, coming from an obscure patent inspector.

Albert looked over at his wife, who was cradling their three-year-old son in her arms. He felt warm and secure. His life was good. He had everything a man could want: a loving family, good friends, and a job that supported him and gave him the freedom to let his mind wander through the mysteries of the universe. Albert was happy with his little life in Bern. Surely he must have known that the papers he had published would change all of that.

CHAPTER EIGHT

Professor Einstein

The morning after his papers appeared, Albert rose before the sun did, which was early even for him. In the bluish pre-dawn glow of their room, Mileva still lay sleeping. The house was quiet, and Albert could hear little besides the sound of his own thoughts.

Albert sat by the window and listened to the chirping of the birds and the other sounds of the awakening world. How he loved to spy on nature in these quiet moments. The sun was just peeking up over the horizon, shooting shafts of golden light through the morning sky. Albert felt the same sense of awe and mystery at the beauty and wonder of nature that he always felt when he saw such things. A smile brightened his face as a familiar thought came to his mind: "It's good to be alive."

Albert stared into the mirror as he dressed. He looked at his soft brown eyes, at his slightly pudgy but handsome young face, and at his curly brown hair, uncombed and wild, as usual. "Not bad," he thought to himself, twirling his mustache. "Not bad, for a man of only twenty-six."

Albert was thinking of his three articles that had appeared in the recent physics journal. The journal lay open on the floor next to the bed, amidst an assortment of socks and other discarded clothing. "Those papers ought to ruffle some feathers," he thought with an impish smile. No sooner had he thought this, though, than Albert's mind raced to a new problem. "Ah, but there is still so much to be done," he mused.

As Albert stood tying his tie, his mind was millions of miles away. It was somewhere near the seething surface of the sun, where the great force of the sun's gravity began its journey through space.

The special theory of relativity created a revolution in physics by revising all the earlier ideas about space, time and matter. But Einstein felt that the revolution was not complete. The theory dealt only with frames of reference that were moving at constant speed in a straight line. What would happen, he asked himself, if a frame of reference were accelerated—speeding up, slowing down, or turning a corner? The problem turned out to be his greatest challenge, and his greatest accomplishment. He solved the problem by taking a completely new approach to the strange force that Newton called gravity.

Newton, in his day, had recognized an obvious defect in his own theory. The theory said nothing at all about how long it takes the gravitational influence to travel through space. It seemed preposterous to believe that something happening at the other end of the universe could affect the earth instantaneously. In the new physics, the speed of light was the upper limit of all speeds. Was it possible that gravitational effects traveled at the same speed? If the sun were suddenly to disappear, would the earth continue to orbit around its ghost for another eight minutes?

Albert dressed more carelessly these days. When he first got his job at the patent office, he was mindful always to dress neatly, like any young businessman. His suit was generally neatly pressed, his tie straight and tacked down with an ebony pin. He would even comb his hair. Now, his position at the patent office was more secure. His bosses had promoted him to patent inspector second class, and had given him a generous raise. He therefore felt he could be more himself. He no longer fussed so much with his clothing. He might wear the same suit for days at a time, along with a wrinkled shirt which he found more comfortable than the ones Mileva starched and pressed for him. His hair was back to its old wildness.

When Albert arrived at the patent office, he was greated by his friend and colleague, Michelangelo Besso. Besso, as everyone called him, was a dark, handsome, man of the world. He was one of the friends with whom Albert spent long hours in the cafes of Bern, talking about physics and Albert's new theories. Besso would sit with his penetrating brown eyes fixed on Albert while Albert explained his ideas. When Albert was finished explaining, Besso would not look blankly and say, "Yes, that's very *nice*, Albert," the way many people would who had not understood. Besso, though not a scientist himself, had a wonderful capacity for listening and a great imagination, which allowed him to understand his friend's soaring thoughts.

Besso would even offer bits of criticism and advice.

Discussions with Besso.

This was quite helpful to Albert, who did not have the luxury of having university colleagues on whom he could test out his theories before writing them up. Besso's main advice was, "My dear Einstein, couldn't you have said all of that more simply?" At such times Albert would smile and shyly agree. Later, people often remarked at the clarity with which Albert wrote about the complex problems of physics. Albert felt he owed much of this ability to Besso's light-hearted contempt for scientific jargon.

Albert was so grateful to his friend for his attentive ear that he mentioned him in his paper on relativity. "I am indebted, for many invaluable suggestions, to my friend and colleague, M. Besso."

Scientific writings are usually full of tiresome references to other scientists. But Albert had only mentioned Besso, an obscure patent inspector like himself.

Besso was sitting at his desk reading the words his

friend had written about him. "You do me a great honor, Herr *Professor* Einstein," shouted Besso as Albert walked into the office. Besso and Albert's other friends had taken to calling him "Professor" lately, as a loving and respectful joke, for Albert was always talking about physics, as any professor of physics might.

Indeed, Albert had been a professor for a little while at least. Before he took his job in Bern he had taught physics part-time at two Swiss high schools. But he had only been a substitute teacher, and the money he earned was not nearly enough to feed and house a family.

The patent office paid him enough money, and he enjoyed the companionship of Besso and other congenial colleagues. But Albert could not help wondering how his work might prosper if he had the stimulation of colleagues who were true scientists, or the resources of a great technical library, with shelves full of the latest books and articles on theoretical physics. These could only be gotten at a university.

As soon as he got home at night, Albert would ask Mileva for his mail. He was impatient to hear some response to his articles, especially the one on relativity. But for months there was nothing, only the usual bills. When he submitted the article, Albert had been certain that someone would take notice, if only to dispute his wildly new theories. But his work was greeted by an icy silence.

Albert went on with his life as before. When he went to work he packed physics problems along with him the way other men packed a lunch. At home, he enjoyed the pleasures of family life. He took great joy in playing with his young son, Hans Albert. There was almost as much of the child in the father as in the son. Albert had a great love of gadgets of all kinds, and he liked to make toys for his son. Once, he made a cable car by stringing together some empty matchboxes. The fact that the cable car really worked impressed little Hans Albert so much that he never forgot the toy, though his father made him many others like it.

One evening Albert came home and didn't ask for the mail as usual. He passed Mileva in the kitchen and went immediately to the woodpile to chop kindling for the fire.

When Mileva went to the window and watched her husband as he swung the large axe, she knew from the look of intensity on his face that he was thinking about some problem in physics. She hoped he would be careful, and that her absentminded husband would not chop off a leg. Albert's expression reminded Mileva of their wedding night, when Albert had forgotten the keys to their apartment. They had had to wake the landlord to let them in. Perhaps even then he had been off in space with his thoughts. "Well, wherever he is, he'll be surprised to see what the mail has brought him today," she thought.

Albert came in and placed an armload of kindling by the coal stove. Then he picked up the coal bucket. As he walked back through the kitchen on his way to the coal bin, Mileva held a letter before his eyes. It was addressed to "Herr Professor Einstein, The University of Bern." Albert laughed his great, hearty laugh, put down the bucket, and tore open the letter. He knew that, finally, someone had responded to his articles, but he would never have expected this particular reply.

Albert looked at the name at the top of the letter: "Herr Professor Max Planck." He was too excited to read on. "Professor Planck, indeed," he shouted with glee. "So, someone has actually taken notice, and a *real* someone at that." Albert expected the letter to be full of criticism, but he didn't care. Max Planck was one of the world's most highly respected physicists. He was the creator of Planck's constant, one of the newest fundamental laws of nature to be discovered, and one of the most intriguing. It was a formula for the release of radiant energy. Albert himself had used this constant to work out his paper on the photoelectric effect, which appeared in the same issue of the physics journal as his relativity paper. Now, the great Professor Planck was writing to *him*.

Albert braced himself for the critical words he was sure the great scientist would hurl at him, but instead he read:

Dear Professor Einstein:

I have read with great interest your papers in the Annalen der Physik on the Theory of Relativity and the Photoelectric Effect. I must say I am fascinated and energized by your application of the speed of light as a universal constant. However, there are some questions I should be pleased for you to answer concerning some of your ideas . . .

Albert could not believe what his eyes told him.

Surely, this must be some joke of Besso's. "Professor Einstein, indeed," he muttered to himself. "That Besso can be a real clown sometimes." But Mileva showed Albert the postmark on the envelope. It had been mailed from Berlin, Germany, home of the great Planck. If Besso had played this joke, he had taken a two-day trip to Berlin and back to do it. Even the impish Besso would not go to such trouble just for a laugh.

Planck's letter boosted Albert's spirits. He now *knew* what he had always believed, that he was a physicist. Planck himself had read and appreciated his work. Even if Planck had quibbled about certain points, what did that matter? More importantly, Planck found in Albert's work inspiration for his own important work. That should be enough to show other physicists that Einstein was a scientist to be reckoned with.

Soon, Albert tried once again to gain a professorship. He applied to be a private tutor at the university in Bern, the first step to a full-time appointment. He submitted his article on the theory of relativity, and other published writings, to the authorities in the School of Physics, seeking to obtain his doctoral degree. He was amazed when they turned him down. Was his theory good enough for Planck, but not for the tiny school at Bern? Apparently, it was not enough. The faculty insisted that Albert write another paper to earn his doctorate and permission to teach in their university.

At first, Albert was too angry to comply with the university's request, but soon he was hard at work, in his odd moments at the patent office, on ideas to include in a thesis for his doctorate.

One day, as Albert sat working in the patent office, a young man dressed in a handsome topcoat and a newly pressed suit walked into the outer office, hat in hand. He peeked into the room where Albert was working and asked meekly, "Can you show me the way to the office of Professor Einstein?" Albert laughed, "I am Mr. Einstein, though I am no professor, at least, not yet." The young man was stunned. He reached out his hand in disbelief to shake Albert's. His thoughts raced. "This fellow, in shirtsleeves, his tie loosened, and up to his elbows in blueprints and patent applications, this is Einstein," he said to himself.

"I am Max Von Laue, assistant to Professor Max Planck," the young man said pompously. "The Professor wishes to send his regards; he is deeply impressed with your work."

Albert rose from his chair and took his visitor's coat. "Tell Herr Planck that I am honored. His is one of the great names in modern physics," he said.

The two men sat and began to discuss physics. As they talked, Von Laue realized that this must indeed be the mysterious Einstein, whose papers contained such amazing new ideas. His grasp of physics was too strong and vast for a mere patent inspector, Von Laue thought.

Von Laue told Albert that Professor Planck agreed with most of the revolutionary ideas in the theory of relativity, but he had some bones to pick with Einstein's photoelectric effect.

A few years earlier, Planck himself had shocked scientists with his discovery that light energy radiated from a heated object is released or absorbed by atoms not in a constant stream, but in separate and distinct blasts, like tiny gunshots. The amount of energy in each of these separate blasts Planck called a "quantum," a Latin word which means "how much."

Albert, in his paper on photoelectrics, said that light energy is not only absorbed in these separate bundles, but that it actually travels through space in them. The word "photo" is Greek for "light." Albert said that light is emitted in bursts of "photons," or particles of light. One such burst of light particles was much like Planck's quantum of absorbed energy. Planck had thought that the absorption of energy in bundles, or quanta, had nothing to do with light, which he still viewed as a wave. Albert claimed that light is absorbed in quanta because light energy travels that way, as a bundle of particles.

Planck, though he had discovered this quantum effect, could not agree with Einstein's conclusions about light. His assistant voiced his objections for him. "How can light be both a particle and a wave, Herr Einstein? It doesn't make sense." Albert smiled and replied, "Don't let the dictionary get in the way of science. 'Particle,' 'wave,' these are merely words. The important thing is to discover the way that nature behaves. In some cases, light acts like a particle. In others, like a wave. I can accept the fact that nature has more than one mood."

Over the next several months, Albert received many other letters and visits from scientists interested in hearing more about his theories. They were all amazed that he scribbled his ideas down in snatches at the patent office, or stayed up late in his tiny study, which was really only a corner of his bedroom, where he surrounded himself with stacks of books and papers.

Soon, Albert had concluded the paper that the University of Bern had requested, and he was granted his doctorate and permission to teach physics part-time.

Albert's first physics class was quite small. It had only four students. The class included his friend Besso, another friend, Maurice Solovine, and Albert's sister Maja, who was living in Bern and attending the university as a student of literature. The job didn't pay much. Albert made only what his students chose to pay him, and since they were his friends, he couldn't ask for much. But Albert liked having his own class, and he took the lessons very seriously.

The class full of friends sometimes resembled Albert's sessions with them in the cafes of Bern. They got into long, animated discussions of physics that lasted much longer than the hour-long class scheduled by the university. This would usually happen when Albert brought up the topic of his own theories, about which he would become especially animated. Once Besso asked Albert to clarify his idea of time. How was it that time was not the same for everyone? Albert answered that time should not be thought of as something that exists *absolutely*. It is only a concept that men apply to the universe to measure phenomena. And, "if the universe were to come to an end tomorrow," said Albert, "then time, and space too, would also come to an end. They have no independent existence."

Albert wheeled from the blackboard where he had been jotting down mathematical formulas to go along with his explanation. He scanned the familiar faces of his "students." Besso, Maja, Solovine, all seemed to share the same blank look, the same rather dumb smile. They wanted to understand, but it *was* difficult sometimes. "Oh well," thought Professor Einstein. "It's a start."

CHAPTER NINE

A Rising Star

After teaching part-time for a year in Bern, Albert received an appointment as a full-time assistant professor at the University of Zurich. Finally, at the age of twenty-nine, he would be able to support his family solely through his work as a physicist.

Albert could scarcely believe that someone would actually *pay* him to study and teach physics. He had always been happy to do it for free. Now he would have access to the books and papers of a good technical library. Now he would be able to converse, not with patent inspectors, but with other physicists like himself. Now, Albert thought with a grin, he would be scribbling notes and formulas not on little scraps of paper to hide in the drawer, but on a blackboard in a classroom.

The time had finally come for Albert to leave the comfortable nest of the patent office. His bosses were sorry to see him leave. He had been an industrious worker. They had even promoted him recently to patent inspector *first* class.

Later, Albert would remember fondly his years at the patent office. They had been some of the most productive and happy of his life. He thought that civil service work was ideal for a young scientist. It removed him from the pressures of university life, where professors must regularly publish new theories or lose their positions. "Publish or perish," went the old saying about university life. Albert thought that an isolated job which gave the young scholar time to think for himself was better to start with—a job like a patent inspector, or, as Albert was to say later, a lighthouse keeper. Such a worker performed a useful function, and still had time to devote to exploring the mysteries of science.

Before he moved his family to Zurich, Albert felt it was time for them to take a short vacation. He had been working hard lately and had not spent as much time with Mileva and little Hans Albert as he would have liked. So the Einstein family traveled to Lake Geneva, the sprawling, clear lake on the border of France and Switzerland. There they went sailing. Albert had loved sailing ever since he was a young boy in Munich, when his father used to take the family out for day-long sails on the peaceful lakes that surrounded that city.

By now, Albert had become quite a seaman himself. He loved the calm and quiet of life on the water. Away from his books and his formulas, his mind and spirit found their true nourishment. Even out on his sailboat, though, Albert always brought along a pad and pencil which he stuffed in his pocket. From time to time, when the lake was calm and the wind was down, Albert would stare out at the water, and occasionally jot down a formula or note in his spidery handwriting.

On the first day out, Hans Albert enjoyed sitting next

Sailing with son and wife.

to his father, and learning how to tie back the sail and turn the rudder that steered the boat. Albert thought he would make a sailor of the boy. Mileva, however, was quiet and moody, sitting in the front of the boat. Albert had noticed that she had been a little distant lately. He thought this trip might cheer her up and bring some color to her cheeks. But she just sat, sullen and sulking, as the boat pierced the clear, shimmering water, the fresh wind filling their sails.

Albert could not imagine what was wrong with his wife. Had he been shutting her out of his life too much lately? Perhaps his mother had been right. Perhaps, Albert thought, Mileva is an unhappy person who will never look on the bright side of things. How could she fail to enjoy the beauty and calm of this lake, he thought.

Perhaps there was another pain tugging at Mileva's heart. She, like Albert, had been a physics student at the

105

university when they met. She, too, had had aspirations to do great things in the world. Now, Albert, who was four years younger than she, was writing theoretical papers. He received letters and visits from many of the greatest scientists of Europe. Just after he quit the patent office, he received an honorary doctoral degree from the University of Geneva. When she married Albert, Mileva had completely abandoned her career.

Perhaps Mileva would have felt better if Albert had shared his work with her, but they never discussed physics. He may have thought she would not be able to understand his ideas, for Mileva had not been a very good student. Perhaps he didn't want to embarrass her by discussing his theories, which even trained scientists often found baffling. Or perhaps he felt that it was not the place of a wife to discuss business with her husband. Maybe he felt that she occupied another part of his life, a place that was lighter and happier than the exacting world of formulas and theories. But Mileva did not seem to be in such a lighter, happier place during this vacation. Each time they went for a sail, she just stared at her feet while the boat sailed on.

That autumn, the Einstein family settled in Zurich and Albert began his duties as a full-time professor of theoretical physics. By now, Albert was becoming something of a celebrity, at least among physicists and physics students. News of his revolutionary papers was spreading in the field of science. Students at Zurich flocked to sign up for his lectures.

Albert quickly became a favorite of the students. He

would show up for class shabbily dressed, wearing un-matched socks and pants too short for him, so that he looked more like a bohemian musician than a renowned physicist. As for the classes themselves, they did not re-semble at all the military-like drills of his own school days. Here, too, Albert the lecturer was more musician than professor. He conducted his classes like an im-promptu performance. He would bring with him one or two index cards on which he had scribbled lecture notes. He would always wait until he got a "feel" for his class, the way a performer takes the temperature of the audi-ence, before he began to speak. He would often abandon his notes entirely and improvise like a jazz musician. When Albert got going on a theme, whether it was on the theory of specific heat or on the paradoxes of space and time in his own theory, he was a virtuoso performer.

Albert quickly gained a reputation as an exceptional teacher. He had a way of explaining difficult concepts using images that were easy to understand. "A man fall-ing freely in the earth's gravitational field who drops an object will not notice it is falling." This famous example illustrates the fact that not only uniformly moving bodies but accelerating ones as well had to be included in the theory of relativity. By painting clear pictures of his ideas in the minds of his students, Albert became one of the most well-loved teachers on campus.

As Albert's popularity as an instructor grew, more and more students signed up for his classes. His magnetic appeal even began to draw students away from the neigh-boring F.I.T., the other Zurich university, which Albert himself had attended. So many students wished to sit at the feet of this great scientist that he had to teach from six to eight hours a week, instead of the four hours that other, less colorful instructors were required to teach. And the extra classes were still filled to bursting!

Albert soon tired of teaching so much. Though he loved physics, he did not enjoy preparing lesson after lesson on the same old subjects. He wanted to be able to follow the whims of his own scientific muse, which often led to dark, uncharted regions of physics, where his students would be quickly lost.

During this time, when Albert was busy planning lectures and teaching, Mileva gave birth to their second son, Eduard, whom they nicknamed "Tedel," the little bear. Now there were further demands on Albert's time, as he had to help his wife care for the children. With all this, Albert still pursued his own scientific work. During the two years that Albert taught at Zurich, he published eleven papers on theoretical physics, and also conducted many experiments. He was so busy, in fact, that he wrote to a friend, "my *real* free time is less than in Bern."

During his years in Zurich, Albert's growing fame among his European colleagues brought him invitations to teach at many other distinguished universities. It also brought him to professional conferences and meetings, where he met many of the leading physicists of the day. Many of these men had reservations about Albert's relativity theory. Though they agreed in general with Albert's explanation, it was hard for many to accept some of the *results* of the theory, such as the fact that the length

"Twin Paradox"—before and after.

of an object that was moving near the speed of light would appear shorter to a stationary observer. Or that to the stationary observer, time on a fast-moving vehicle would look as if it had slowed down.

This latter case suggested the "twin paradox." According to Albert's theory, if a man flew into space in a rocket going near the speed of light, and returned after, say, 40 years, he would appear to have aged only slightly, whereas his identical twin who had remained on earth would be old and wrinkled. This was due to the slowing down of time for the man on the rocket. Such results, which had not yet been supported by experiments as they since have been, rubbed many classically trained scientists the wrong way. They felt that Albert's theory was more like science fiction than science.

Albert met these objections by saying that the conclusions of his relativity theory were not mere "tricks." Instead, they revealed the way nature works at very high speeds. He was helped by the support that men like Planck gave to his theory. However, it was many years before most of the world's physicists accepted the theory.

After two years of teaching in Zurich, Albert got an appointment as a full professor of theoretical physics at the University of Prague, in the part of the country of Austria-Hungary that later became Czechoslovakia. Albert was growing tired of his burdensome load of courses at Zurich. Even though he loved Switzerland, he wanted a change. The University of Prague offered a promotion and a larger salary to Albert, who now had another mouth to feed. However, the job offered Albert something else of importance. The university, Albert wrote to a friend, had "a fine institute with a large technical library." Albert also wrote to his friend, "The students here are not as intelligent and industrious as the students in Switzerland." However, this was probably a plus for the young theorist, for the students in Zurich ate away at the valuable time Albert needed for his work. They would gather in a circle around him after class to ask questions. He could never refuse to answer; it was not in him to be rude to students. Memories of his own harsh treatment at the hands of German teachers was still too fresh. In fact, far from being rude, he would often invite a group of students out to a coffee house after class, where the discussion from the class would be continued. Though these talks were rewarding fun for all concerned, they were time consuming. It would not be surprising if Albert welcomed a roomful of "not as intelligent" students, who would perhaps ask fewer questions.

Mileva seemed unhappy in Prague. For one thing, Switzerland had become her home. She had lived there through her four years in college, and for several years after in Bern and in Zurich. It was difficult for her, with a new infant, to be uprooted to a strange place, away from her friends and loved ones. This move, which must have seemed unnecessary and unfair to her, put a strain on the marriage.

While in Prague, Albert continued his work on relativity. His first theory had to do with bodies moving in *uniform* motion, motion that does not change its speed. This he called the special theory of relativity. Now, he wished to extend his theory to cover *accelerated* motion, the motion of an object that is gaining speed. This, too, he wished to show, was not absolute, but depended on the frame of reference of the observer. Albert called his work to extend the special theory the general theory of relativity. It was to occupy him for many years.

Extending the special theory to accelerated motion was a difficult problem, for the concept of the relativity of motion did not seem to apply to acceleration.

For instance, in the case of a moving train that has no windows, an example physicists love to use, a person riding on the train would not know it was moving as long as the speed remained *constant*. He would not see trees or landscapes going by. Therefore, if we assume a perfectly smooth ride, the passenger in the train might well believe he is standing still. This is a classic example of the relativity of motion. Uniform motion cannot be detected within a given frame of reference.

However, if the same train accelerates or picks up speed very rapidly, or slows down or turns a corner, then the passenger will feel the shift. He will lurch backwards or forwards, and his head may even strike a hard blow on the headrest. He now knows that the train is moving, even though he cannot *see* any relative frames of reference, such as trees and landscapes flying by. This is why acceleration is said to be *absolute* motion. One does not have to judge it *relative* to any other reference points.

This apparent nonrelativity of accelerated motion bothered Albert. He wished to extend his theory of relativity to cover *all* motion.

During his days in Bern, Albert had puzzled long and hard over this problem after the publication of his special theory. Finally, one day, while he was sitting at his desk in the patent office, an idea occurred to him that he later described as "the happiest thought of my life." A person falling freely in a gravitational field would not know there is any field there at all. On the other hand, a person accelerating in outer space might think he is in a gravitational field.

To explain this idea, Albert used the simple example of an elevator, in an infinitely tall building, that had broken free of its cable and was hurtling downward at faster and faster speeds. The people on the elevator would be falling at the same rate as the elevator, and they would seem to be floating freely in space, above the floor of the elevator. It would be the same to them as if their elevator were out in space, beyond the reach of the gravity of the earth. If they were to drop something in the elevator, a watch or a pencil, these objects, too, would seem to be floating freely before them, but they would actually be accelerating downward along with them and the elevator. Thus, Albert had shown that accelerated motion too was relative to the frame of reference of the observer. For these observers would have had no way of knowing that they were falling down an elevator shaft in the earth's gravitational field unless they were able to look outside, at the floor markers on the building as they whizzed past them.

When Einstein thought of his elevator in free space, he might not have imagined that such a thing could actually happen. It has. A space craft in orbit around the earth does not have its engines on. Traveling in orbit is a kind of free-fall. The astronauts and everything else inside the space craft are in a state of "weightlessness." They float around freely inside the cabin. It is as though gravity had been turned off in that frame of reference.

Albert next brought his elevator out into space. There, he attached it to a collossal fishing line which was reeling in the elevator very quickly. The elevator is now being pulled, not falling, and thus the people in it will now be able to stand on the floor. To them, this acceleration seems merely like the normal force of gravity at work on earth. This effect can easily be seen in an ordinary elevator. If a 160-pound man is standing on a scale in an elevator, the scale reading might go up to 180 pounds when the elevator starts upward. It could drop to 140 pounds as the elevator comes to rest at the top.

Next, Albert supposed that while the elevator is being pulled through space, a beam of light is shone through a hole in one side. The beam of light would enter in one place, but since the elevator is accelerating quickly upwards relative to the passengers, the beam of light would strike the opposite wall in a slightly lower place. This, Albert said, is the normal effect on light as it passes through a gravitational field. Light, he claimed, would be bent as it passed through such a field.

What Albert had shown with these "thought experiments" is the equivalence of a gravitational field with acceleration. He had shown that acceleration of the frame of reference produces effects that are exactly the same as those produced by a gravitational field. If you were inside the elevator, you could not tell whether the elevator was accelerating or the whole system was at rest on some large planet. This was a very powerful extension of his special theory.

Next, Albert proposed something very daring. He said that his theory could be proven by experiment. He had shown, at least in his rocketing elevator, that a beam of light would be bent as it passed through a gravitational field. He now proposed that this effect be measured in nature. He said that starlight would bend in a specific angle as it passed by the sun.

Albert's theory was a whole new way to look at gravity. He thought that it need no longer be thought of as a force. Rather, gravity should be explained as a curvature in the geometry of space. Motions in space are controlled not by the attractions of a force, said Albert, but by the curved paths surrounding material bodies in the geometry of space.

Though the sun is too bright to enable observers to detect starlight passing by it during the daylight hours, Albert thought that experimenters could take a picture of the stars around the sun during a total eclipse, when the moon would cover the sun and allow the starlight to be seen. A comparison of these eclipse photos with a photo of the same stars when the sun was in a different part of the sky would show whether the light from these stars was bent as it passed by the sun. If this were true, Albert felt his general theory of relativity would be supported.

Albert arranged with an astronomer, Erwin Freundlich, to test his theory. Freundlich was to travel to the south of Russia in 1914 to photograph the upcoming eclipse of the sun. Though Albert was confident that the test would prove him right, he was still quite curious to see just what those photos would show.

CHAPTER TEN

The Roving Professor

There were times when even Albert had to get dressed up. He stood before the mirror of the hotel room as Mileva straightened his stiff, white collar, and tied his black bow tie. Tonight was to be a very big event—a formal reception and dinner for the top physicists of Europe.

Mileva, in her flowing evening gown, was helping the squirming Albert get dressed. He was not being co-operative. To him, putting on a pressed shirt was like going to prison. On top of that, tonight he was donning a starched collar, a bow tie, and tails. To Albert, it must have seemed like solitary confinement in a strait-jacket.

With Albert finally dressed, the Einsteins strolled down the long, winding stairway of the stately old hotel. A group of elegantly dressed scientists milled about, arm in arm with their wives, in the spacious lobby spread with lush oriental rugs. Huge crystal chandeliers hung overhead, and the high ceiling was draped with bunting.

This gathering, which the Einsteins attended shortly after they moved to Prague, was the first of a series of meetings called the Solvay Conferences, named after the man who funded them, the millionaire Ernest Solvay. This man, besides having patented his own process for the manufacture of washing soda, sodium carbonate, had a passionate interest in physics. Solvay felt that it would be a good idea, during these times of radical changes in physics, for the top physicists in the world to put their heads together.

By now, Albert was getting accustomed to traveling among the top scientists of Europe. After all, he was one of them. In fact, many people said he was the most ingenious scientist living. Albert, of course, would have denied it. He respected the work of his colleagues too much to have felt superior to them. Indeed, much of his own work was based on the labors of some of the men who were in the room that night. He was indebted, for example, to the thin, gray-bearded H. A. Lorentz, the father of the Lorentz transformation rules. Einstein owed a lot to Lorentz, who had first produced the formula for contraction of a moving object. Lorentz explained this contraction on the basis of his electron theory. In Einstein's relativity theory, the same formula became a way of expressing the change from one frame of reference to another.

Albert also knew that many of the men milling about the room and discussing the physics of the day were a bit troubled by his special theory of relativity. They still could not get used to things like clocks slowing down, or lengths shortening, when the frame of reference was different. They could not accept that measurements were not absolute, as they had been in the mechanical theories

117

of Newton. To them, relativity was merely a bag of magic tricks, not a revelation of the way the universe worked, as Albert strongly contended.

Fortunately, Albert was not alone in defending his theory. The strong voice of Max Planck was also often heard in these hallways, arguing for the soundness of Albert's ideas. Indeed, Planck often compared Einstein to the great scientists of the past, particularly to Copernicus. Copernicus believed he had shown that the sun, not the earth, is the center of the universe. In modern terms, he had simply changed his frame of reference. The motions of the planets, it turns out, are simpler to understand when the frame of reference is the sun rather than the earth.

Planck maintained that Einstein was a modern Copernicus, for Albert had shown people once again that their point of view, their perspective on the universe, must be altered. In Copernicus' time, it meant looking at the Earth as a small speck in an immense universe, not as the center of the universe. In Einstein's modern world, it meant not relying absolutely on measurements taken from one perspective. Planck felt it was a great achievement. Many others would think so, too, when all was said and done.

The Solvay Conference was a huge success. The scientists discussed the most important new work in physics being done in their day. They paid particular attention to the quantum theory, first developed by Planck and his follower in the field, Albert Einstein. This field was beginning to uncover a strange new split personality of nature—such as the fact that light behaved sometimes as a particle, and sometimes as a wave.

Albert made the closing speech of the conference, summing up the latest developments in the quantum theory. By all accounts, his presentation was a success. One of the scientists present, Marie Curie, a French chemist and physicist and the co-discoverer of radium with her husband Pierre, said of Albert that she "appreciated the clearness of his mind, the shrewdness with which he marshaled his facts, and the depth of his knowledge."

Apparently many of the scientists at the conference shared her feelings, for Albert soon was even more sought after than before. Universities all over Europe, in Holland, Germany, and even Albert's old school, the F.I.T. in Zurich, were making him offers of professorships. Now it was felt that to have Albert Einstein on the faculty was a great plus.

Albert had chosen to leave Prague a few months after his arrival. It is odd that he accepted the offer of a professorship at the F.I.T. It was only 12 years before that the faculty members there had denied him a recommendation to become a professor. Many of these same men were now fawning over him to get him back. One of them, the brilliant mathematician Herbert Minkowski, had once called Einstein the student "a lazy dog." Now Minkowski welcomed the lazy dog back home, as perhaps the most respected physicist in the world. Ironically, Minkowski himself developed the system of mathematics that Albert used to express his general theory of relativity.

Albert spent two years teaching at the F.I.T. Mileva

was happy to be back in Switzerland, after the bleak, lonely months in Prague. Albert, meanwhile, was reunited with his old college friend Marcel Grossman, whose careful class notes had saved him from failing his exams. Marcel was a mathematician now at the F.I.T. During these years, Albert and Marcel began a long collaboration. Marcel helped Albert work out the complex mathematical formulas that were to make up the general theory of relativity.

After only two years back in Zurich, the Einsteins were on the move again. Max Planck came to Zurich and persuaded Albert to take a post at the new Kaiser Wilhelm Institute for physics in Berlin, Germany. Planck told Albert that the scientists there, and the Kaiser himself, the supreme ruler of Germany, wished Albert to be the director of the new institute. This would mean, among other things, a much higher salary, and relief from teaching, for Albert would have no regular classes. He would only have to make an occasional address. On top of this, Albert would be made a member of the Prussian Academy of Sciences, the most prestigious scientific association in the world.

Albert thought over this offer. It was quite tempting in many ways. The chance to do only theoretical work had always eluded him. Now, he could have all the free time he wanted to develop his theories, as well as the opportunity to keep close tabs on new developments in physics. His colleagues would be among the best physicists in the world.

There was one main drawback. Taking the offer

would mean moving back to Germany, to Berlin, the stronghold of the stern and narrow-minded Prussians that Einstein had loathed since his days as a schoolboy in Munich. To make matters worse, there was talk of asking Albert to become a German citizen again. Therefore, Albert made it a condition of his acceptance of the appointment that he be registered as a Swiss citizen and as a Jew. This was doubly significant, for Jews in Berlin were being widely persecuted at the time.

In spite of Mileva's opposition to the move, the stubborn Albert decided to accept the post of director of research at the Kaiser Wilhelm Academy of Physics. He felt he could not afford to pass up such a high salary for a position that would give him a great deal of freedom and no teaching responsibilities. The post was, in many ways, ideal for Albert, who had a great many problems in physics to think through. This appointment would afford him enough time and the right environment in which to develop his theories. At the age of only thirty-five, Albert felt lucky to have it.

There was one thing more. Albert was now working on some of the most complex aspects of his general theory of relativity. He needed people around him who understood the direction of his thoughts. Such men lived in Berlin. As one of the top scientists of the day, Rudolph Nernst, was to say, "Only a dozen men in the world understand relativity, eight of them live in Berlin."

Of course there were drawbacks. After all, Albert had renounced his German citizenship almost 20 years earlier. The reasons he had done it still existed. If anything, the Germans in Berlin were even more rigid and regimented than the ones in Munich.

The move to Berlin was toughest on Mileva. She preferred the casual, happy atmosphere of Zurich. The somewhat bleaker atmosphere of Berlin was not at all to her liking.

Berlin was a place where order meant everything. Taste meant nothing. Food tended to be flavorless and dull, but filling. Women tended to dress for duty rather than beauty. They wore mud-brown homemade skirts, plain hats, baggy, shapeless coats, and square-toed boots. What a boring, lifeless bunch of scrubwomen they looked like. Mileva did not want to end up like one of these Berlin women.

Social life for the Einsteins was not very interesting, either. There seemed to be a set of unwritten laws for behaving in public that could not be ignored. Germans tended to belong to strict social circles, and one circle was not supposed to overlap with another. The wife of a jeweler would talk to the wife of a jeweler, not the wife of a doctor; and a doctor's wife would generally not speak to a tradesman's wife. To do these things would invite disorder, which the regimented Germans preferred to avoid. To the Einsteins, the Germans' extremely orderly lives were quite boring. There is evidence that even the Germans themselves found this so. According to one visitor to Germany at about the time the Einsteins moved there, some Germans ate seven meals a day out of sheer boredom, just to have something to do.

Soon after the Einsteins relocated to Berlin, the fis-

Living alone after marriage breaks up.

sures in their marriage became deeper, until a break became inevitable. Mileva could not tolerate life in a colorless, crude Berlin, no matter what her husband's career required. Within weeks of their arrival, Mileva took the children and moved back to Switzerland.

Though Albert and Mileva did not officially divorce for many years, they were never reunited. Albert was left alone in Berlin. He soon moved into a small bachelor apartment. Now he had nothing left but physics.

CHAPTER ELEVEN

Life During Wartime

Albert now forgot himself in his work. He made preparations for his friend Erwin Freundlich's projected expedition to the south of Russia to photograph the eclipse. He planned the activities of the Kaiser Wilhelm Physics Institute, which he now directed. Above all, he set his mind to mastering the mathematical puzzles of his general theory.

It was during this period of his life, after Mileva and the children had moved and he lived alone in his small apartment in Berlin, that the quirky side of Albert's personality began to assert itself.

Albert had never cared much for what other people thought of how he looked or acted. He never went along with conventions. Now that he was a bachelor again, and one with a job that afforded him much freedom, Albert cared even less than ever what people thought of him. He seemed to be lost in his own little world of mathematical formulas and musing on the vast universe.

One evening, at the end of a cozy dinner with his friend Erwin Freundlich and Mrs. Freundlich, Albert did something that became quite characteristic of him. In the midst of a discussion of physics with Erwin, as the house-keeper cleared the table, Albert took out his pencil and began scribbling formulas on the tablecloth. It was a family favorite brought out only for company. Mrs. Freundlich was aghast, but she said nothing.

Erwin advised his wife never to wash that tablecloth. He felt that when Albert became famous, which he was sure to do, his fame would change the tablecloth from a household item into a collector's item. Mrs. Freundlich washed the tablecloth, anyway. However, later she might have wished that she had listened to her husband. Today, mere scraps of paper bearing the doodlings of Einstein sell at auctions for thousands of dollars.

Soon, Erwin packed his telescopes, gathered his cameras and set off on the expedition to the south of Russia to photograph the eclipse. Finally, thought Albert, here was a chance to test an aspect of his theories. They had always seemed to be valid on purely logical grounds. Now, Albert's work would be measured against nature herself. If he was correct, it would be evident for the world to see. If he was wrong, he would have to abandon his theory.

The final test was not to be. Germany declared war against Russia while Freundlich and his team were there, setting up their equipment. Now, Freundlich, a German, was on *enemy* soil. He was soon arrested and put in jail. During wartime, even the innocent star-gazing of astronomers seems ominous. Freundlich was released shortly thereafter, but the eclipse had already come and gone by then. The testing of Albert's theory would have to wait.

Soon, Germany also declared war on France, and invaded Belgium, a neutral nation like Switzerland. When Germany did this, England declared war on Germany to protect the rights of the neutral country and to offer some resistance to Germany's aggressiveness.

Albert read the daily headlines in horror. Not only was his expedition spoiled, but Europe and the world beyond seemed to be going mad. Everywhere, it seemed, the people of the world wanted war. Albert had watched Germany since he was a little boy, and her present belligerence and bullying were no surprise to him. But the people of other countries now caught war fever, too.

In Germany, this mood of war-hysteria was exhibited in the cult of the Kaiser, Wilhelm II, the absolute ruler of united Germany. Albert remembered hearing about a speech the Kaiser had made when he first came to power. After taking his oath of office, the Kaiser did not thank the people gathered in the great square to cheer him. He didn't even look at them. Instead, he turned to the soldiers, who stood sternly at attention in their blue Prussian uniforms, and said: "My army. We belong to each other, I and the Army; we were born for each other."

Albert would never forget what the Kaiser said next. It was as if he had been there himself. He could almost see the Emperor's face turn fierce and steely as he shouted, "If your Emperor commands you to do so, you must fire on your father and mother. There is only one master in the Reich, and that is I. I shall tolerate no other."

The Kaiser.

Such was the devotion that the Kaiser expected from a German soldier, and the German soldier obeyed. In fact, most Germans—military or civilian—gave the Kaiser full support in his fanatical militarism.

The Kaiser and his army placed themselves above the common people. It was just this sort of militarism that had made Albert give up his German citizenship as a young man. Now, the situation was worse than ever. The Kaiser, in his flowing cloak and shining white helmet, was treated like a sort of demi-God. Army officers were only slightly less exalted. In fact, a person overheard insulting an officer could be arrested and imprisoned.

It is no wonder that when the Kaiser called Germany

to war, his nation happily obeyed. Cheering crowds of people lined the streets as the soldiers marched in heavy goose-steps out of town toward combat. Everyone seemed to want this war. Albert watched as the madness unfolded around him. He felt sometimes as if he were the only sane man in Berlin. He had never seen such an eagerness and lust for war and blood among a people. One young army officer summed up the feelings of the country when he said, "war is like Christmas." War was seen as a holiday for a people with a strong army and a strong will. Albert shuddered when he heard such madness. What, he wondered, would become of a world where people felt this way?

Albert had always known that the common people in Germany could be swayed by a brightly colored uniform and the military bravado of the Kaiser and his army. However, he felt that his colleagues in science were above these blood lusts.

Albert believed that scientists, in their search for truth, could not help but understand the truth about war—that it is the most tragic, futile undertaking anyone could engage in. He felt his colleagues would refuse to support this war, and any war, just as he had chosen not to support it. Albert was to learn how wrong he was about his fellow scientists.

Scientists were only too eager to help build the German war machine. In fact, it was the contributions of scientists to the ghastly art of battle that made this war— World War I—different from any other war that had occurred before.

In rapid succession during the years prior to the war, scientists developed new instruments of death. The small bore rifle fired a bullet farther, faster, and more accurately than older rifles. It used a smokeless powder, which meant that soldiers no longer had to wait for the thick, billowing smoke of the battlefield to blow away. They could fire, and still sight their enemy clearly for another shot.

Thanks to the greater range and cleaner operations of modern rifles, a pair of armies could begin killing each other while they were still far apart. They would not even have to look each other in the face. War was now becoming less personal. It could be fought long distance.

The magazine-loading rifle made reloading a snap, so that six times as many bullets per minute could be fired by the modern soldier. Even more shots could be fired by the new machine guns. They became a tool for the mass production of corpses on the battlefield as they burped out showers of bullets. Later, bombs planted underground, or dropped from high-flying planes, also delivered massive doses of death such as the world had never seen before.

Since German technology and research led the world, Germany had built more of these new weapons than any other nation on earth. In the newspapers Albert read with horror of the ingenuity of the Germans when it came to killing. How could his fellow scientists justify their researches into these new engines of destruction and death? He had supposed them to be on the side of the angels, seekers after truth—thinkers of God's thoughts, like himself. But they, like most men, were only too glad to respond to Germany's call for violence on an international scale. Albert thought these men were mad to support Germany in this war merely because they were Germans. To Albert, Germany was, quite plainly, wrong to have started the war in the first place. He hoped that Germany would be defeated, but he was wise enough to keep his hopes to himself.

Many of Albert's scientific colleagues were so convinced of the rightness of Germany's cause that they tried to win the war with their pens as well as their inventions. They wrote a manifesto to convince the people of the world to surrender because Germany "deserved" to win the war. This was called the "Manifesto to the Civilized World."

The manifesto denied Germany's war guilt for having invaded Belgium. It argued that there was no choice for the Germans but war and victory if German culture, the greatest culture the world had ever known, were to survive. This ridiculous document, which tried to justify the unjustifiable, was signed by 93 of Germany's most prominent scientists and intellectuals.

Albert was shocked at the stupidity of his colleagues for becoming puppets of the Kaiser and his gang of uniformed thugs. His shock turned to anger when one evening he read of the horrible happenings at Ypres in Belgium. There the German army opened the valves on over 5,000 cannisters of a new poison gas developed by Max Nernst and other German scientists. The deadly stuff was called mustard gas.

Gas warfare.

The use of mustard gas in World War I was one of the first uses of "chemical warfare" in Europe. The horror of using chemicals to kill and maim assaulted Albert from the pages of the daily newspaper. On that night, a greenish-yellow cloud gradually formed in Ypres from the 5,000 hissing cannisters of gas opened by the German troops. One of the Allied soldiers on the scene said, "There were men running away and we didn't know why."

Two whole divisions of French soldiers panicked and fled. This left a five-mile-wide gap in the Allied lines. Others who could not escape the fumes were lying comatose in the mud, clutching shreds of clothing to their faces to shield their breathing. Five thousand men died in only 40 minutes, and 5,000 more were captured.

Since the gas could not be aimed like a bullet, it often

reached civilians as well. Some estimate that as many as one and a half million civilians were affected by mustard gas during the war. The effects of the gas were seared, scarred lungs, wheezing and coughing, and shortness of breath. These effects remained for life, that is, if the gas did not kill.

Albert decided that it would be wrong just to sit idly by while his colleagues supported the madness of German aggression. He felt that someone must take a stand for civilized people. Someone had to show the world that there were people in Germany, and in all of Europe, who had not succumbed to the hysteria of war.

Albert teamed up with a friend to write the "Manifesto to Europeans." In it he pleaded with sensible citizens of Europe to realize that the continent was not made of several separate countries, but of one vast, interconnected people. He called for a united Europe of peace and cooperation. He claimed that, with the network of technology and trade that already joined the nations of Europe, they really were already one country.

This brave call for reason and good faith fell on deaf ears. Only four other professors signed it. Though Albert was somewhat safe from injury as a Swiss citizen and a prominent scientist, his colleagues and the government began to look on him as something of a nuisance.

Life in wartime Berlin was not very pleasant for Albert. His pacifist views set him at odds with almost all of his colleagues. This made it even more difficult for him to adjust to life as a bachelor. Before, he had always

Convalescing in bed and writing.

had someone to take care of him. Now, when outside pressures were at their peak, he found himself alone. Without the help of a wife, it was difficult for Albert to balance his intense theoretical work with his normal, everyday needs for nourishment and sleep. Before long, Albert fell ill with a severe stomach ailment that kept him bedridden for months.

Albert's doctor described his haggard existence at this time by saying, "As his mind knows no limits, so his body follows no set rules. He sleeps until he is wakened; he stays awake until he is told to go to bed; he will go hungry until he is given something to eat; and then, he eats until he is stopped."

During the first two months of his illness, Albert lost 56 pounds. He was wasting away and in need of care.

It was fortunate for Albert that living in Berlin at this time was his distant cousin and friend from boyhood, Elsa.

During this time, Elsa, too, had been recently divorced and was living with her two daughters. Elsa was a kind, cheerful woman who readily filled the role of caretaker for the convalescent Albert. This closeness helped the two to do more than just renew the easy friendship of their youth. Elsa eventually nursed Albert back to health, at which time he moved into her home and became a kind of father to Elsa's two grown daughters. In time, when Albert's divorce to Mileva was made final, Elsa and Albert would marry.

Elsa's easy manner and cheerful disposition were just what the doctor ordered. She organized all of the household details that were so arduous for the abstract thinking Albert. She cared first for Albert the man, not the scientist, for she had no real interest in science as Mileva had had. This eliminated any of the competitiveness that once existed between Albert and Mileva. Indeed, Albert once wrote to a friend that he felt "glad my wife doesn't know any science. My first wife did."

As Albert convalesced in his sickbed, a copy of his paper on general relativity reached the hands of a prominent British astronomer and physicist, Sir Arthur Eddington. Even though Albert was an "enemy" scientist, Eddington was wise enough to realize that Albert's ideas were sound and deserved his fullest attention. He quickly arranged for a team of photographers to take pictures of the upcoming solar eclipse in May 1919, to test the bending of starlight predicted in Albert's theory.

While Albert was recuperating from his illness, the Kaiser's Germany was perishing from its own peculiar virus. The war was going badly on all fronts. The United States had entered the fray, helping to push the beleaguered German forces back from where they had come. The highly touted German U-boats were all but annihilated by the British navy. The end of the war was near at hand.

On November 9, 1918, Kaiser Wilhelm ruefully abdicated the throne of Germany. A new government was proclaimed from the steps of the Reichstag, the German lawmaking assembly, on the same day. Soon, an armistice was signed establishing peace. Albert wrote to his mother in Switzerland, "The great event has happened."

The Einstein Cigar

I n the darkroom lit only by a dim, red bulb, the scientist slid the photograph paper into the pan of developing fluid. The paper curled slightly around the edges. Then, in a few moments, images began to appear: tiny dots surrounding a bright, shining rim.

The scientist was developing a photograph of the stars surrounding the sun, taken during the recent solar eclipse, when the sun's blinding light was covered by the moon.

When the photograph was dried and compared with an earlier picture of the same stars, taken when the sun was not near, the results seemed clear. The stars were in a different position in the earlier photograph. Their light had "bent" when it passed by the sun. The sun's gravity had attracted the starlight, and, as it turned out, the angle of the starlight was exactly as Albert Einstein had predicted it would be. There was only one possible answer. Einstein's general theory of relativity had passed its first crucial test.

The news spread quickly. Newspapers around the

world carried headlines much like the one that appeared in the London *Times* on November 7, 1919:

THE SCIENTIFIC CONCEPTION OF THE FABRIC OF THE UNIVERSE MUST BE CHANGED

Almost overnight, Albert Einstein had become the most famous scientist in the world. He was already well known among the scientists of Europe for his earlier work. Now his name was on the lips of common people as well, even people who had very little understanding of the complex ideas of science. Everyone seemed eager to learn what the shaggy-haired scientist had to say.

In his expanded theory, Albert said that accelerated motion, motion that changes speeds, is *equivalent* to gravity. This meant that acceleration is also "relative" motion, for a frame of reference is needed to tell if gravity or acceleration is at work. One has to look out of the speeding elevator, at another frame of reference such as planets moving past, to see that the elevator is being pulled through space. One needs something to relate to the motion of the elevator before one understands that gravity is not at work, but acceleration.

Albert also said that gravity is a product of matter. The effect of the gravity of material objects is to "curve" the space around them. Just as the beam of light curved as it passed through the moving elevator, objects passing by a material body in space will follow a curved path. Albert said that this would be true even for starlight, and the photos taken during the eclipse proved him right.

Since even before the time of Newton, it had been assumed that the shortest path between two points was a straight line. Now, Albert had shown that things did not work that way in outer space. In space, it is often true that the shortest path between two points is a curved line, as shown by the bending path of the beams of starlight.

Albert had redrawn the map of space. It was now seen to be curved around planets and stars, due to the force of gravity of those objects, which creates a sort of cosmic suction that bends the very fabric of space. The daring and originality of this theory stunned the world of physics. One scientist called it "the most beautiful product of scientific thought."

Einstein's new theory of gravity solved the problem that had bothered Newton 200 years earlier. The complex mathematical formulas of general relativity, written with the help of Albert's friend Marcel Grossman, told how the gravitational effect travels through space. It moves as a gravitational wave, at the speed of light. Today, elaborate experiments are being planned to find these gravitational waves.

Though news of a stunning new vision of the universe quickly circled the globe, normal people sometimes had trouble understanding what all the fuss was about. Newton's theories, which were taught in just about all the schools of the world, had seemed to explain well enough how the universe operated. They had been able to predict the motions of the planets and stars and the effects of the force of gravity.

General relativity immediately gave an answer to a problem that had been bothering astronomers for a century. The planet Mercury was behaving abnormally. Its orbit was changing in a way that could not be accounted for by Newton's law of gravity. It was a very tiny change; the planet was being displaced, every year, by an angle equal to the thickness of a pencil line seen from a mile away. It seems like a very tiny problem, but to an astronomer, it was one that had to be explained. It turned out to be exactly what should be expected if the curvature of space were taken into account. Astronomers were delighted. Einstein had given them a theory that they could use to calculate the motion of heavenly bodies with greater accuracy.

Since scientists were very excited by Albert's theories, people generally felt as if they should be excited too, and they became very curious about them. They felt as if these new theories had changed their lives, though they were often at a loss to say just how.

There was something else that made people curious about Albert's theories. In 1919, the world was very weary of war. Every day for years the newspapers had been filled with gruesome accounts of the senseless, bloody fighting in World War I. Now, this new theory, by a German scientist, proven with tests done by Englishmen, the recent enemies of the Germans, gave the world something hopeful and marvelous to think about. It was not long ago that Englishmen had been murdering innocent dachshunds, simply because these dogs had a German name. Now they were cooperating with a former enemy scientist. What they discovered helped the world to lift its eyes from the muddy battlefields of Europe to the soaring planets and the distant stars.

Newsstands and bookstores were soon flooded with articles and books explaining both aspects of Einstein's theory of relativity. Only one year after the theory passed the test of the eclipse photos, over 100 books and numerous articles had appeared. By the year 1987, those numbers were into the thousands and still growing.

Albert could have gotten rich with all of the offers he received from newspapers, magazines and book publishers for his own account of his theories. However, he used restraint. He only wrote two articles that first year, for distinguished publications. Later, he published a book on his theories for the nonscientist. People soon realized that Albert's explanations of his own theories were often much clearer than the writings of other experts. He had not forgotten Besso's sound advice about clarity.

Even with all of the explanations of the theory that appeared in the press, many people still misunderstood it, especially Albert's concept of "relativity." When people couldn't understand how the idea applied to scientific measurements, they tried to apply it to life in general, where it seemed easier to understand. The phrase "everything is relative" became very popular. It was thought to mean that nothing is better than anything else; that one person is as good as another; that one idea, one style of music, or one plate of food, is just as good as another, since, as everyone now knew, "everything is relative."

But this sort of relativism was the furthest thing from Albert's mind when he created his theory.

Albert had not sought, in this theory of relativity, to prove that *everything* is relative. Rather, in the words of the great philosopher, Bertrand Russell, he sought to "exclude what is relative and arrive at a statement of physical laws that shall in no way depend upon the circumstances of the observer." Albert tried to find absolutes in science by *getting rid of things that were relative.*

The more people misunderstood the theory, the more their curiosity seemed to grow. Albert quickly became the focus of their interest. If they couldn't understand the theory, they could certainly understand its author.

Promoters quickly tried to capitalize on the public's curiosity about Albert. The London Palladium music hall said it would pay Albert whatever he wanted to appear on its hallowed stage for a three-week engagement. The managers of the hall were not clear just what sort of "show" they thought Albert could put on. He declined their invitation.

Mothers named their children after the famous physicist. Albert became one of the favorite subjects of newspaper cartoonists, who loved to draw the "absent-minded professor" with his faraway look and wild, wiry hair. One tobacco company even put out a new line of smokes to capitalize on Albert's burgeoning fame called "The Einstein Cigar."

Albert's house was besieged by the press and curiosity seekers. Whenever he walked out the door he was surrounded and hounded for interviews and pictures. The popping of flashbulbs and the shower of questions hurled at him by reporters became part of his daily routine.

Albert's every movement was watched. His phone rang constantly. It seemed to him as if the world had suddenly gone crazy, not as it had during the war, but in a whole new way.

Albert didn't particularly enjoy all of the fuss. Soon after news of the eclipse photos broke in the press, Albert wrote to a friend and told him that the attention he was getting was "so bad I can hardly breathe, let alone get down to any sensible work."

CHAPTER THIRTEEN

Loved and Hated

A lbert and Elsa's formerly peaceful home life was now the eye of a hurricane of publicity that surrounded the suddenly famous physicist. Each day the mailman would drop off large sacks full of letters. There were letters from scientists wishing to congratulate Albert, from promoters wishing to make money showing him off, and many letters from little children.

For a time, Albert tried to answer some of the letters. He especially tried to answer the letters from children.

One little girl wrote asking the great Einstein for help with her math homework. A little boy wrote to ask if he understood Albert's theory of the relativity of motion correctly. "Does it mean that if I were moving in empty space, that I couldn't tell if I was moving, because there would be nothing to be moving *away from?*" wrote the little boy. Albert wrote back to the little girl and tried to show her how to do her homework, without giving her the answer. He wrote a long letter to the little boy, congratulating him on how well he had understood the complex theory.

It soon became obvious to Albert that if he were to read and answer his ever-growing mountain of mail, he would not have the time to do anything else. Albert had to settle for answering what letters he could and filing the rest.

Albert slowly realized that there was no escape from his sudden fame. He and Elsa therefore decided to make the best of it. Now, when newspapers asked for photos of Albert to go along with their endless stories about him, they had to pay a fee for them. The money was given to poor children.

Albert also received many requests from groups of people who wanted the help of his famous name and reputation to raise money for their causes. He decided to help the people whose causes he shared. Albert had always been a pacifist; he felt that war was senseless. He therefore agreed to give lectures for pacifist organizations which could raise money by selling tickets to see the famous physicist. Albert also agreed to help Jewish organizations in this way. He felt that the persecution of Jewish people in Germany and throughout Europe meant one thing: that the Jewish people needed a homeland of their own where they could escape the hatred and prejudice of other men. Albert agreed to help Zionists, people who sought to establish a Jewish homeland, by going on a lecture tour and soliciting money for their cause.

Soon Albert and Elsa embarked on a series of worldwide tours to put Albert's fame to productive use. They traveled through Europe and to America and Asia. Some of Albert and Elsa's most peaceful moments during these times, when the eye of the public was constantly on them, were spent on the long sea voyages to far-off lands.

Disembarking on first trip to the United States.

Albert had always loved sailing and the sea. Looking out at the vastness of the ocean reminded him of something important. He felt, as he said during his first boat crossing to America, "dissolved and immersed in Nature" when he looked out at the endless chopping waves of the sea. It reminded Albert of the insignificance of any one man in comparison to the grandeur of nature; that he himself was not so important as the world was making him out to be. Such a thought "makes one happy," he said.

The Einstein's quickly awoke from such dreamy thoughts when their ship docked in New York. The American public was hungry for news of the famous physicist, and the publicity machine was geared up to give the public what it craved. At the docks that day, thousands of people had waited for hours to greet the visiting physicist. When they saw Albert standing atop the gangplank, holding his briar pipe, with his violin case under his arm, they erupted in cheers and applause.

When Albert and Elsa walked down the gangplank, they were greeted by the popping of flash cameras and a barrage of questions from reporters, who scribbled down everything the couple said. Often, the questions were downright silly. A favorite was, "Professor Einstein, could you explain briefly for our readers your theory of relativity?"

A less patient man might have refused to try to explain "briefly" the work of over 15 years of intense thought. However, the amiable Albert did his best. He took a slow draw on his pipe, and looking calmly out over the sea of eager reporters and spectators, he said, "The theory shows that time and space are not absolute and exist only where there is matter. Thus, when the universe ceases to exist, time and space will also cease to exist."

Albert smiled wryly as the reporters frantically scrawled his words into their notebooks. He had meant this answer to be something of a joke, though there was truth in it. But the reporters trumpeted Albert's over-simplified answer to the world as a revelation. Headlines proclaimed:

EINSTEIN SEES END OF TIME AND SPACE

Taken out of context, this proclamation seems to suggest that Albert was predicting the end of the universe.

He had only meant to say that time and space should not be seen as absolute entities, but as relative measurements.

Many times during the Einsteins' tour of America the press made similar misrepresentations of Albert's statements. Sometimes, they misunderstood him and printed false information. Once, after Albert had finished a lecture to a group of college students on the topic of light, the headlines trumpeted:

EINSTEIN SAYS SPEED OF LIGHT CHANGES ACCORDING TO SPEED OF SYSTEM MEASURED

Reporters thought Albert had said the speed of light is *not* constant, which was exactly the opposite of what he said. His theories are based on the fact that light always travels at a constant speed. If this most basic idea was misunderstood by the press, Albert felt he had little hope of being understood in America.

Though the American press may have had trouble with Albert the scientist, they soon learned to appreciate Albert the man. His shabby style of dress and mussed up, shaggy head of hair, his air of vulnerability and innocence, and his wry and ready smile softened the hearts of journalists.

Reporters presented a picture of Albert to the people that was part true and part fantasy or myth, but the myth was soon accepted as the reality. One story recounted that Albert was so forgetful of worldly things that he had once used a $1,500 check as a bookmark and lost the book.

Another story had Albert forgetting his glasses and asking his waiter to read the menu, only to be told, "Mister, I ain't had no education either." Such stories of Einstein the vulnerable, Einstein the inconspicuous and Einstein the unassuming charmed the people and sold a lot of newspapers. These tales made people believe that Albert was one of them. He was viewed as the most American of scientists: soft spoken, warm and patient, and not the least bit pompous or pretentious. In short, Albert was seen as a sort of people's scientist, and in America a man of the people is always warmly received.

After their tour of America was over, Albert and Elsa traveled across the globe to Japan and to many other countries. In each of them they were greeted warmly and Albert was showered with praise and honors.

In 1921, shortly before arriving in Japan, Albert learned that he had won the Nobel Prize for physics. Albert was awarded this prize for his work on the photoelectric effect. This may reflect the doubts that many physicists at the time still had concerning Albert's theory of relativity. However, the photoelectric paper is a masterpiece in its own right, since it opened the door to the quantum world, a frontier of physics that will be explored for generations to come.

Albert arranged to give his prize money, which was a very large sum, to his former wife Mileva, to provide for her and his two sons. This helped him ease his feelings of guilt about his unsuccessful marriage, and assured that his children would be well cared for. Mileva would never have to work to support them.

People the world over had opened their arms and their hearts to Albert and Elsa, but on their return to Germany, the Einsteins received a very different reception. Many Germans still felt bitter and humiliated by their recent defeat in World War I. Germany was still reeling from the loss of the vast amounts of money spent trying to fund the huge war effort. Now, money was tight, and people were growing desperate and uneasy. They wanted someone to blame for their problems.

Some Germans felt that the country had been weakened by people who had not supported the war—pacifists, intellectuals, and Jews especially. Albert was all of these things, and he became the focus of the frustration that his countrymen were now feeling. In Berlin, large public meetings were held to denounce Albert and his theories. Ignorant men claimed that no Jewish person could ever arrive at a true physical theory; only "Aryan" German minds could think like that. Albert's theories were labeled, contemptuously, "Jewish physics."

Albert realized that the attacks on him and his work were ignorant and unfounded. The best scientific minds in the world had tested his theories and approved them, but that didn't stop the critics. They called meeting after meeting to denounce Albert. There were even rumors that Albert's life was in danger, that he would be assassinated to avenge Germany's honor, which he supposedly had tarnished. This was surely twisted thinking, for Albert had brought honor to Germany in his travels to all the corners of the globe.

Albert chose not to hide from his tormentors. One

evening, a large anti-Einstein rally was held in Berlin. Speaker after speaker led the large crowd of spectators in vicious attacks on Albert's theories and character. In the midst of this hateful scene, a new spectator shuffled into the hall and took a seat near the front. The crowd instantly recognized the shaggy-haired man sitting there as Albert Einstein himself.

As the speakers railed on and on with their ridiculous accusations, Albert sat back and laughed out loud. The more preposterous their claims, the louder he laughed. The people in the audience could not believe their eyes. How was it, they thought, that Albert dared to enter this lions' den of his enemies? No matter what they thought of him that night, many of the people in the audience could not help but admire Albert's courage. He had not allowed threats of assassination to stop him from getting a good laugh at his enemies' expense.

Albert did what he could to restore his country's faith in him. He even became a German citizen again, though he was later to regret it as "the biggest folly of my life." For, no matter what he did, many Germans would not give him peace. They needed a scapegoat to blame their failures on, and the peaceful physicist was an easy target.

Albert did not allow his critics to distract him from his work for long, however. Now that he had expanded his theory of relativity, he wished to work on another bothersome problem. Albert had always believed in the unity of nature, which is why he felt that relativity must hold true for all motion, not just constant motion. Now,

Albert felt that nature's unity must be understood by physics in a whole new way.

Quite properly, Einstein felt himself to be in the mainstream of physics. In the whole history of the subject, there had been a trend toward the unification of ideas. Faraday found the relationship between electricity and magnetism, and Maxwell brought light into the same picture. The relativity theories had united gravitation with acceleration and mass with energy. The author of these unifying ideas now set out to finish the job. He would find a "unified field theory." This was to be a complete theory of physics, joining the knowledge of gravitational and electromagnetic waves into a single theory. The subatomic world and the most distant reaches of the universe would be described in the same set of equations.

This was certainly a colossal task, even for a physicist as great as Albert, who had already proven himself the equal of Newton, perhaps the greatest physicist in history. The *New York Times* reported what Albert's theory would attempt to encompass:

the wheeling of the planets, the speeding of light on its course, the attraction of earth for a falling stone, the luster of the diamond, the instability of radium, the lightness of hydrogen and the heaviness of lead, the flow of electricity through a wire, millions of manifestations of matter, energy, time, space.

Albert was attempting to find a theory to unify all

of the forces of nature. It was a large task that was to consume the rest of his life.

While Albert worked on his unified theory, work continued on the quantum theory. Physicists had been uncomfortable ever since Albert had discovered that light exhibits aspects of both a wave of energy and a particle of matter. In 1923, French physicists Maurice and Louis de Broglie added a little more strangeness to the question. They said that light is not a particle sometimes and a wave sometimes. Rather, they said, light is a particle of matter *guided* by a wave of electromagnetic energy.

Then the brothers de Broglie really shocked physicists. They said that not only is light constructed of particles guided by waves, but *all of matter* is so constructed. Electrons, protons, and every other body are made up of particles of matter guided by waves of energy.

These ideas would have been ignored had it not been for Albert Einstein. He recognized in them an important truth about the dual nature of physical reality, and because of Albert's interest, physicists began to pay a great deal of attention to the de Broglies' ideas. However, these ideas were to lead physicists down a road which Albert would not follow.

Soon, a young Austrian physicist named Erwin Shroedinger came up with a new theory. He said that matter is not particles guided by waves. Rather, Shroedinger said, everything is made up of waves of energy which intersect or cross each other. The point where the waves meet is a particle. "The particle is made up of many waves that cancel each other out except where the particle is," said Shroedinger.

Next a man named Werner Heisenberg claimed that these waves must be called "waves of probability." He said that one can never calculate exactly where a particle will be, or how fast it will be moving, but one can only say that it will probably be in a certain place, based on Newtonian mechanics, and that it will probably be moving at a certain speed.

Heisenberg called this idea the "uncertainty principle." It was to have a great impact on the development of science in the twentieth century. Like Albert's theory of relativity, Heisenberg's principle of uncertainty had to do with scientific measurements.

Heisenberg claimed that one could not even merely look at life in the subatomic, quantum world without changing it. Take, for example, the case of a physicist trying to measure the position of an electron, or its speed. In a very simplified sense, to look at the electron the physicist would have to shine a sort of light on it. Normally, the lighting of an object takes place when a stream of photons, or light particles, hits the object, for light is made of streams of photons. However, when a photon hits a tiny electron, it knocks the electron out of its position and changes its speed. Thus, at this tiny level of nature, even looking at things, by shining photons of light on them, changes them.

Scientists felt that they had run up against a boundary of nature. There seemed to be phenomena that could not be measured with certainty, because they could not even be looked at without changing them. Of these things one could only say that one thing or another was probably true. Using sophisticated mathematics, one could say certain very probable things about particles and waves of matter and energy, but they were still only probabilities. The certainty that had been the basis of science was gone.

No physicist was better qualified than Einstein to deal with the new, probabilistic approach to physics. As early as 1900 he had published papers in the field of statistical mechanics. This is a mathematical theory about the motions of molecules. With so many trillions of molecules in a single drop of water, there is no way to figure out what each one will do. The best the physicist can do is tell what a molecule will *probably* do. Statistical mechanics is a way of figuring out what will happen by averaging all the probabilities. Einstein wrote 40 papers in this field, including his 1905 paper on molecular motion. One of his other papers tells why the sky is blue. A theory he developed in another paper provided the basis for the invention of the laser. His paper on the theory of specific heats of metals set dozens of physicists off into a new field, which is now called solid state physics. Nearly every field of physics felt the impact of Einstein's statistical methods.

The new field of quantum mechanics, the theory of particles, began when Einstein applied his statistical method to light. This is what earned him the Nobel prize for the 1905 paper on the photoelectric effect. For the next twenty years, he was one of the leading architects of the theory. His last important paper, in 1925, used statistical methods to make an important distinction between two classes of particles. Any book on quantum mechanics now defines a boson as a particle that obeys Bose–Einstein statistics.

From the beginning, Einstein felt that the statistical approach could not be the whole story. The method is useful in dealing with molecules, but Newton's mechanics tells *exactly* how each molecule moves in its interaction with others. The basic laws of motion are not probabilistic. Einstein felt that the same thing must be true in quantum mechanics. The most a physicist can now say about a radium atom, for example, is that it will probably disintegrate some time within the next 1,600 years. Knowing this, he can calculate how many will break up in the next hour. But Einstein believed that physics must look deeper. There must be some law, he said, that will tell us when any given atom will fall apart. "God," he said, "does not play dice with the universe." He set physicists of the future the job of finding the rigid laws that lie behind the probabilities of quantum mechanics. So far, there is no hint that there are such laws, and physicists today are convinced that the laws of the fundamental particles will always be probabilistic. That is why Nils Bohr once told Einstein, "Albert, stop telling God what to do."

As he aged, Einstein continued to make contributions to many fields of physics, but without the brilliance that marked his earlier work. In the last decade of his life, he published eight papers on unified field theory, but he never succeeded in producing a finished theory. Others continue to try. He also published biographical material

Collapsing on ice due to illness.

about other physicists, and several works on the philosophy of science.

In 1929, the long years of hard work and infrequent physical exercise caught up with Albert. One day, while carrying a heavy suitcase through slippery snow, Albert collapsed. His doctor diagnosed a weak and infected heart. It took Albert a full year of rest to recuperate, and he never really regained his former vitality. Even in sickness, though, Albert continued his work. He seemed to enjoy the undisturbed atmosphere of his sickroom. "Illness has its advantage," he said. "One learns to think; I have only just begun to think."

As theories of uncertainty swept through the scientific community, an uncertainty in the hearts of men was also making itself felt in the world. Germany, and later the entire world, went through a disastrous economic collapse called the Great Depression. As people across the world waited on bread lines for meager meals, a new and evil force raised its head in Germany, promising to bring back prosperity. This force was the German Nazi party, and it reawakened the visions of military glory and world domination that had been sleeping in the souls of Germans since the end of World War I.

Albert watched from his window as a troop of Nazis paraded their message of hate to the desperate German people. He could see that the old German madness was on the rise again.

CHAPTER FOURTEEN

Fought with Sticks

On the evening of May 10, 1933, a torchlit parade of thousands of students marched to a square next to the University of Berlin. There, before the halls of learning and inquiry, the students made a great stack of books and lit them with a torch. The flames ate quickly through their precious fuel, turning what was once a record of wisdom and thought into a ferocious bonfire. One book, at the top of the stack, was almost completely eaten through by the fire. On its blackened spine these words could still be read: "The Meaning of Relativity, by Albert Einstein."

As the flames grew and flickered in the frenzied fates of the crowd, Nazi soldiers led the people in wild chants. "Down with non-German thought. Down with lies and falsehoods," they ranted wildly as the crowd cheered.

Besides Albert's books, the works of the greatest authors in the world were burnt that night in Berlin and in many other cities in Germany. The Nazis were spreading their hideous ideology of hatred for everything non-German, which in reality meant anything that ran counter to the vision of the Nazi leader, Adolph Hitler.

Hitler had convinced the downtrodden German people that their problems would be solved by rebuilding their long-dormant armed forces, and by ridding their society of the people who had held Germany down. To Hitler, these problem people were the intellectuals, pacifists, and Jews. He had an insane hatred for Jews, and like many before him, he blamed them for most of the ills suffered by the Germans. He persecuted the Jews as they had never been persecuted before.

After he came to power in 1933, Hitler isolated the Jews from the mainstream of German life. He forbade marriages between Jews and so-called Aryans. He excluded Jews from public office, the civil service, journalism, radio, farming, teaching, the theater, and films. He kicked them out of the stock exchanges, and barred them from practicing law or medicine, or engaging in business of any kind.

Not only were Jews prevented from earning a living, but they even had a hard time buying food and clothing. Many shops could now be seen with signs saying "Jews Not Admitted" plastered over their doors. Pharmacies would not sell drugs or medicine to Jews. Hotels would not give them lodging. On the outskirts of many towns were signs reading: "Jews Strictly Forbidden in This Town," or "Jews Enter This Place at Their Own Risk." Such signs often even carried sadistic and cruel jokes. One roadsign read, "Drive Carefully! Sharp Curve! Jews 75 Miles an Hour."

Fortunately for Albert, he was visiting the United States when Hitler came to power. If he had been in Germany, it is likely that Hitler would have had him killed or imprisoned. Albert was the most visible and outspoken

Under the Nazis in World War II, Jews are persecuted.

of the hated Jews and intellectuals in Berlin. As it was, Hitler's troops raided Albert's vacant house, rifled his papers and belongings, and seized his bank accounts and financial assets. Hitler charged Albert with being a spy, and many say he put a price on Albert's head. To many Germans during that horrible time, Albert Einstein was worth more dead than alive.

Albert soon realized that he could not return to Germany. He therefore publicly renounced his German citizenship once again, and scolded his colleagues in the

Prussian Academy of Sciences for standing idly by while their Jewish colleagues were cruelly persecuted by the insane Nazi regime.

Albert accepted an offer to come to the United States to live. Princeton University in New Jersey wanted him to become a resident at its new Institute for Advanced Studies. Albert was asked what salary he would require. When the Princeton administrators saw the low figure he named, they tripled it. Financially secure, and with a position that granted him much freedom to continue his research, Albert was safe from the terror of Nazism that was stifling so many other German scientists, especially Jewish ones.

As the years passed, Albert watched from afar as the virus of hatred grew and consumed his former country. Finally, the Germans occupied Poland in the horrifying "Blitzkrieg" or lightning war, of 1939. The other European powers had had enough by this time. England and France declared war on Germany. Russia and the United States would follow them in an alliance against Hitler. World War II had begun. It soon became obvious to the peace-loving nations of the world that if Hitler were not stopped, democracy and freedom itself might vanish from the face of the earth.

Meanwhile, scientists in the United States were concerned about a new development in atomic physics. An Italian physicist, Enrico Fermi, had succeeded in creating a new element by bombarding uranium atoms with a newly discovered atomic particle, the neutron. Soon, German scientists discovered that when they bombarded an atom of uranium something happened that Fermi had not noticed—the nucleus of the atom was split. Scientists discovered that the newly split atom sent out other neutrons. If these were arranged so that they would split other atoms, sending out other neutrons and splitting still other atoms, it was clear that a tremendous chain reaction would ensue. Suddenly, Albert's formula, $E = mc^2$, took on an ominous significance, for it predicted the enormous explosive force that would be unleashed if the power locked within the atom were set free.

When Albert learned of these new developments, he quickly understood the danger faced by the free world. At the urging of a group of foreign scientists who were refugees from Hitler's persecution, Albert wrote a now-famous letter to the president of the United States, Franklin D. Roosevelt. Dated August 2, 1939, Albert's letter said:

> Sir: Some recent work . . . leads me to expect that the element uranium may be turned into a new and important source of energy in the immediate future. . . . it is conceivable . . . that extremely powerful bombs of a new type may . . . be constructed. A single bomb of this type, carried by boat or exploded in a port, might very well destroy the whole port together with some of the surrounding territory . . .

Albert went on to point out that the Germans already had enough uranium and competent scientists to construct several bombs. Albert urged that research in the

United States be taken up quickly to develop such a bomb before Hitler did. Nothing less than the fate of the civilized world was at stake.

Albert was forced to relinquish his life-long pacifism. He now felt that war, at least this war, was the only way to divert the horrible consequences of a world ruled by a madman like Hitler.

Scientists in the United States did not consult with Albert on the development of the atomic bomb. It was felt that he was too old and too outspoken to be trusted with the sensitive secrets of atomic weapons technology. However, Albert did play a role in the Allied war effort. He became an adviser to the Navy on explosive devices. Albert could hardly believe that he was the same man who, only a few years earlier, had said he would "unconditionally refuse to do war service . . . regardless of how the cause of the war should be judged."

Though Albert's views on war had changed for the moment, in other ways he was still stubbornly the same. He was received as a scientific eminence in Princeton, but he continued to dress like a bohemian, even more so than before. Albert still wore the same jacket for days at a time, and he let his shaggy hair grow wilder than ever. He also got into the habit of going without socks and suspenders, giving him the overall appearance more of a disheveled old farmer than a guru of physics.

Albert's friend and collaborator of these years, Leopold Infeld, summed up the physicist's personal habits. "We are slaves of bathrooms, Frigidaires, cars, radios, and millions of other things," Infeld said. "Einstein tried to reduce them to the absolute minimum. Long hair minimizes the need for the barber. Socks can be done without. One leather jacket solves the coat problem for many years. Suspenders are superfluous, as are nightshirts and pajamas. . . . Shoes, trousers, shirt, jacket are the only very necessary things," Infeld concluded.

During these years, Albert became something of a lonely, though colorful, figure in his small, white-shingled house in Princeton. A few years after the move to America, Elsa died after a long illness. Albert found it hard to adjust to life without his wife and fond companion who had done so much to make the pressures of his life easier to bear.

The same year that Elsa died, Albert's good friend and collaborator Marcel Grossman passed away. Albert's loneliness was eased somewhat when his sister Maja came to live with him in Princeton. She took care of the household, as Elsa had before her, and the two shared many long, intimate talks late into the evening. Maja brought out the humorous side of her brother as no one else could. Once, while Albert was working for the Navy, she asked her brother if the Navy planned to put Albert in a uniform. She knew what his reaction would be. The thought of wearing a "ridiculous" military uniform caused Albert to erupt in spasms of laughter.

Albert also loved to tease his sister. Maja was a vegetarian, for she had a tender and loving regard for all animals. She could not bear the thought of killing and eating one. However, she did have one weakness—hot dogs. Once, when Maja had an overwhelming craving for a hot dog, Albert wanted to ease her guilt. He smiled a broad smile and said, "Maja, I believe that in your case, it would be proper to assume that a hot dog is a vegetable."

During these later years in his life, Albert seldom left Princeton. He was happy, after a life full of travel, to be settled down. He had even come to suspect that the joys of travel were illusory. Once, in a discussion with a young friend, Albert said, "I used to imagine far-off places and they were pretty and interesting in my mind. But, when I saw them, they usually were disappointing. My images of them were more exciting." Thus Albert, more than ever, enjoyed above all else the life he lived in the quiet laboratory of his own mind.

Albert's preference, especially later in life, for thought over experience came to light in many ways. Once, the son of a colleague presented Albert with a curious toy, a little mechanical bird that sat at the edge of a bowl of water and kept dunking its head and raising it from the water, as if in perpetual motion. All at once, the little boy in Albert peeped out from under his shaggy gray hair. He was curious to find out how the toy worked. He spent a long time just sitting and staring at the bird. Finally, he propounded a theory. It had something to do with gas in a tube within the bird inflating and deflating it to make it move.

Even before Albert was finished with his explanation, he looked at his colleague's son and said, "No, I guess that's not it." When the boy suggested that they simply take the bird apart to see how it worked, Albert frowned. He would rather return to his mental laboratory to perform further experiments. How else, he seemed to suggest, would it be any fun?

Albert continued with his life happily enough, even though the world outside was engaged in a horrible war. In 1945, the Germans were finally defeated, before they could master the secret of atomic energy. However, the war with Japan, one of Germany's allies, raged on. In 1945, Allied scientists finally perfected an atomic bomb. The Americans decided that the bomb should be used against the Japanese to save the lives of thousands of American and Japanese soldiers who would surely perish if the war dragged on.

But the cost of saving those lives was dear.

On August 6, 1945, the United States dropped an atomic bomb on Hiroshima, Japan. The deadly mushroom cloud that bloomed high in the air above the city after the impact could be seen from 50 miles away. Whole buildings were instantly leveled by the whirlwind created by the colossal blast. The brightness of the explosion was so great, buildings that still stood were "sunburnt"; eerie shadows were etched on walls where the light from the blast was blocked. Thousands of people were killed instantly. Others, trapped under charred debris and earth, died more slowly from the radiation created by the bomb. As the radiation took effect, people's hair fell out and their skin peeled. This was a new kind of horrible death, delivered in massive doses.

In times gone by, humankind had feared four things that could annihilate the human race: war, famine, pes-

Atom bomb.

tilence and disease. These were called the "Four Horse-men of the Apocalypse." Now, a fifth horseman was mounted on his black charger: nuclear weapons, whose power could turn a world to dust and ashes.

A few days after Hiroshima was destroyed, the Americans dropped another atomic bomb on Nagasaki. The destruction was just as swift and horrible. When Albert heard of these ghastly events on the radio, he turned to his secretary and caretaker, Helen Dukas, and said wearily, "Alas . . . My God. That is that."

Albert felt that mankind had finally found a way to destroy itself. It saddened him, but what ate away at his soul even more was that he felt responsible. He believed

167

his development of the equation $E = mc^2$, and his letter to Roosevelt suggesting research on the atomic bomb, were instrumental in the destruction of two cities and over 100,000 lives. What was worse, now that the atomic bomb had been given to the war-hungry world, there was no taking it back. It would be a force to reckon with forever, until people learned to cope with this horrible weapon, or until they destroyed themselves in a final nuclear conflagration.

Albert regretted having written the letter to Roosevelt, which he felt ushered in the age of nuclear war. Had he foreseen what would happen, he may not have done it. Later, in speaking of the letter to a colleague, he said, "It is impossible to foresee the results of what you do. The only wise thing to do is to take no action—to take absolutely no action."

Albert's sadness after the war was heightened when the ghastly truth of the Holocaust began to be known. Survivors of Nazi death camps told of the horrible slaughter of millions of innocent men, women, and children, most of them Jews. This was Hitler's perverted "final solution." His hatred of Jews drove him to lengths that shocked a world already numbed by years of violent death on the battlefields. Albert was so horrified at the Germans' murder of innocent Jews that he swore never to have anything to do with Germany. "The crime of the Germans is truly the most abominable in the history of the so-called civilized nations," he wrote. Since his youth, Albert had known the madness his countrymen were capable of, yet he was still shocked at the horrors of the Holocaust.

After the war, Albert worked tirelessly to get the nations of the world to put controls on the spread of nuclear weapons. He also made many appeals to the nations of the world to form a world government, to insure that the selfish aims of separate nations would never again lead the peoples of the world to murder each other. Albert's pleas for a world government were laughed at. His appeals for controls on nuclear weapons went up in smoke when the Soviet Union soon began testing its own atomic bomb. Now, when Albert pleaded for controls on the development of new bombs in the United States, he was accused of disloyalty. Surely, raged Albert's critics, he must see the Soviet threat and the United States' responsibility to match it. Albert could only see the coming arms race between the two nations, possibly followed by a devastating nuclear war. If such a war were to occur, the next war to follow it, Albert wrote, "will be fought with sticks."

Throughout all of this new activity, Albert still found the time for his final great labor in physics. A few years after the end of the war, he published the last version of his unified field theory. However, the theory was highly speculative, and the mathematics were so intricate that the theory was untestable. Scientists did not take it very seriously. They were making many advances with the new uncertainty principle in subatomic physics, and they felt that Albert's work was simply out of step with the times. Indeed, most scientists today believe that the quantum realm is ruled by probabilities and not by certainties.

Albert continued to dispute the quantum view, but his voice grew softer and softer. Even he seemed to doubt that certainties could be found in the tiniest realms of matter and energy. "Who knows," he wrote to a friend about quantum theory, "perhaps God is a little malicious." Despite his doubts, Albert never gave up trying to find a basis in certainty for quantum measurements.

In 1948, Albert was stricken with a serious recurrence of his heart ailment, which required surgery. He was in weak health thereafter. The doctor became one of his most frequent visitors. Once, a doctor visited a preoccupied Albert to give him some medicine. Albert took the medicine to make the doctor happy. The medicine made Albert nauseous, and he vomited almost immediately, after which he looked up at the doctor and barked, "There, do *you* feel better now?"

In 1951, Maja passed away. Now, with his wife and sister gone, Albert felt more alone than ever before. Still, he continued working every day.

In March 1955, Michelangelo Besso, Albert's friend from his days in Bern, also passed away. Albert wrote to Besso's family that "He has gone a little sooner than me." Less than a month later, Albert suffered a serious recurrence of his illness. The doctors wanted to operate, as they had before. Albert sternly refused. He did not want his life to be "artificially" prolonged. He wanted to die "with some dignity," he said.

On April 17, weak and in great pain, Albert phoned

his secretary from his hospital bed and asked her to bring him writing material and "my most recent calculations." Though the shadow of death hung over him, he still thought of his work.

On April 18, 1955, Albert passed away. He was cremated, in accordance with his final wishes, and his ashes were scattered in an undisclosed place. Albert did not want to be buried in a cemetery, where, he felt, people would make a shrine of his tombstone. However, he could not keep scientists from making a monument of his life's achievements in science.

Physicists today still base more of their original work on Albert Einstein's ideas than on those of any other scientist. His theories are full of milestones of human achievement. He was the first scientist to prove conclusively the existence of molecules. He established the constancy of the speed of light in the universe. He unlocked the secret of atomic energy with his $E = mc^2$ formula. His theory of relativity is the basis for our modern understanding of the universe. His work on the photoelectric effect helped to spawn ongoing work in quantum physics, and led to such inventions as television, the laser, and photovoltaic cells that produce solar power. Even in failure, Einstein may have succeeded, for scientists are still searching, though on a somewhat different path, for a theory to unify the forces of nature in one set of mathematical equations.

Some were quick to judge Albert a failure in his often-thwarted attempts to develop a unified field theory. However, there is more to the matter. Albert himself recognized the difficulty of his task. He admitted to friends that his chances of success were slim. However, he felt that the attempt had to be made, if only to spare other physicists from making the same errors that he eventually made. Albert felt himself uniquely suited to the task of pursuing the elusive theory. After all, his scientific reputation had been made. A younger person, who had yet to make his way in the world, could not risk a career in such unpromising search. Einstein thus felt that it was his duty, as a famous scientist with nothing to lose, to continue the quest for the unified field, a quest which other scientists continue today.

Albert's pursuit of his vision of a unified field theory typifies the approach he took to his work his whole life long. To him, science was more than a collection of experimental results. It was a way of looking at the world with a certain insatiable curiosity, with the same sort of wonder that he felt as a young child when he got his first compass.

When Albert was a child, he felt that to be a scientist meant to "think God's thoughts." In order to do this, he felt, a scientist had to take a leap of the imagination. When he was older, Albert explained that scientists must learn to take imaginative leaps in order "to catch, in a wildly speculative way," a glimpse of the universe as it really is, and not as it merely appears to our crude senses and instruments.

Albert was a scientist with the temperament of an artist. He brought to his scientific work the love of the quest for truth for its own sake, as well as a sense of the beauty of nature. He always felt that a good theory was one that possessed at least some of the beauty and symmetry he found in the world around him.

It is largely because of his artistic temperament that Einstein was among the greatest scientists of the century. His theories touched men great and small, and recast thought in science as well as philosophy. Anyone who sees further along the road to scientific truth in years to come will do so only from atop his strong, broad shoulders.

Alternating current (AC)
a kind of electricity that flows in two directions at once, or, more specifically, that changes its charge from positive to negative very rapidly. Ordinary household current is AC, and changes its charge 60 times per second.

Ammeter
an instrument for measuring electric current in amperes.

Amperes
a measure of the rate of flow of electric current.

Atom
the smallest unit of an element. Scientists used to believe that the entire universe was made up of these tiny particles, and that no smaller particle was possible. Today we know that atoms are made up of many even smaller particles.

Constant
something unvariable or unchanging. A constant can be used as something against which to measure other things that are changing.

Direct current (DC)
a kind of electricity that flows in one direction only, or that keeps the same charge. This is the kind of electricity supplied by batteries.

Dirndl
a style of dress worn in Germany that has a narrow waist and a full, gathered skirt.

Dynamo

a device that generates electricity; a generator.

Electromagnetism

magnetism created by a current of electricity.

Electron

one of the particles that make up an atom. Electrons carry a negative charge and orbit the nucleus of the atom.

Energy

the capacity for doing work. Energy comes in many forms including mechanical energy, nuclear energy, electromagnetic energy and heat.

Ether

an element that was formerly believed to fill all space and to transmit waves of light.

Gravity

the attraction between two bodies, which increases with their mass and nearness to each other. It is this attraction between the earth and every piece of matter on its surface that makes things fall downward.

Laboratory

a place equipped to conduct experiments and scientific research.

Liter

in the metric system, a measure of capacity equal to about one quart

Mass

a measure of the amount of matter contained in a body. In a gravitational field, the mass of a body causes it to have weight. Outside a gravitational field, such as in space, a body is weightless, but still has mass.

Matter

material substance that occupies space and has mass.

Molecule

a specific combination of atoms that creates a substance with specific properties. For example, two atoms of the element hydrogen and one atom of the element oxygen join together and form one molecule of the substance water.

Motion

act or process of changing place; movement.

Neutron

one of the particles that make up an atom. Neutrons carry no electrical charge, and are present in the nucleus of the atom.

Nobel Prize

every year in Stockholm, Sweden, a panel of judges awards this prize to the people who have benefited humanity in the greatest way in various areas, including science, literature, medicine and peace.

Nucleus

the positively charged central part of an atom, usually consisting of protons, neutrons and other particles.

Physics

a branch of science that deals with matter and energy and their relationship to each other. Included within this branch are the fields of mechanics, acoustics, optics, heat, electricity, magnetism, radiation, atomic structure and nuclear phenomena.

Quantum theory

the theory in physics based on the idea of the subdivision of radiant energy into finite tiny parcels called "quanta" (singular: "quantum"). This concept is applied to processes involving the transfer or transformation of energy between atoms or molecules.

Radiation

energy which is emitted in the form of waves or particles, such as heat and light. (This word is often used to mean specifically the harmful radiation emitted by radioactive substances.)

Radioactivity

the property of spontaneously emitting radiated energy, possessed by certain elements, such as uranium and radium.

Relativity, general theory of

Einstein's special theory expanded to include the concepts of gravitation and acceleration.

Relativity, special theory of

Einstein's theory explaining the relation between mass and energy. Expressed mathematically, this is: energy equals mass times the speed of light squared (or $E = mc^2$).

Speed of light

the speed at which light travels (186,000 miles per second). Einstein's theory states that this is a constant, and that nothing can ever travel faster.

1. What kind of a child was Albert Einstein? How was he different from other children his age?
2. What did Albert Einstein mean by a thought experiment? From your reading of the book, describe one of Albert's thought experiments.
3. Why did Albert Einstein find school in Germany dull? What kind of school do you think Albert Einstein would have liked?
4. How was the way Albert Einstein thought about time different from the way most people thought about time? How do you think his theories changed our ideas about time?
5. What did Albert Einstein's father do? Do you think this influenced Albert to become a scientist?
6. In the book the author says that Albert Einstein had the mind of an artist although he was a scientist. What do you think the author means by this? How is the job of the scientist and the artist similar? How is it different?
7. What is it that physicists study?
8. From your reading of the book, try to describe what Albert Einstein said in the special theory of relativity. You may draw a diagram if you like. Why do you think this theory is so hard to understand? How does it contradict what we "see" around us in everyday

life? How, in your opinion, did this theory change the way we understand the universe?

9. Is there such a thing as absolute motion?

10. Why did Einstein reject the idea of there being an invisible substance, "ether," in space?

11. What did Einstein assume about the speed of light in the special theory of relativity?

12. According to the "principle of equivalence," what two things are equivalent?

13. What did the increase in mass of an electron moving at speeds near the speed of light show?

14. From your reading of the book, explain why the statement "everything is relative" is an inaccurate summing up of Einstein's Theory of Relativity?

Adler, Irving. *The Story of Light.* Harvey House, 1971 (Discussion of relativity, pp. 102–110.)

Balton, Sarah K. *Famous Men of Science.* Crowell, 1960

Burlingame, Roger. *Inventions Behind the Inventor.* Harcourt, 1947 (The idea of this book is that inventing is a social process rather than the act of an individual. Includes material on Albert Einstein.)

Dank, Milton. *Albert Einstein.* Franklin Watts, 1983

Fermi, Laura. *The Story of Atomic Energy.* Random House, 1961 (A dramatic account from the ancient Greeks to the present day.)

Freeman, Mae. *The Story of Albert Einstein: The Scientist Who Searched Out the Secrets of the Universe.* Random House, 1958 (This readable account reveals Einstein's personality, but does not explain his theories.)

Goudsmit, Samuel A. and the editors of Time-Life books. *Time.* Time-Life Books, 1969 (Well-illustrated discussion of relativity, pp. 144–165.)

Hammontree, Marie. *Albert Einstein: Young Thinker.* Bobbs, 1984

Kondo, Herbert. *Albert Einstein and the Theory of Relativity.* Franklin N. Watts, 1969 (This work explores both Einstein's work and his lifelong crusade for peace.)

Riedman, Sara. *Men and Women Behind the Atom.* Abelard-Shuman, 1958.